T0198938

SOMETIMES,
SOME PEOPLE &
SOME THOUGHTS

The 40 Day Devotional

A Contemporary Journal of Spiritual
Wisdom & Insight

By

Ivory Stone

authorHOUSE®

AuthorHouse™
1663 Liberty Drive
Bloomington, IN 47403
www.authorhouse.com
Phone: 1 (800) 839-8640

Published by AuthorHouse 11/06/2019

ISBN: 978-1-5462-6333-3 (sc)
ISBN: 978-1-5462-6332-6 (e)

Library of Congress Control Number: 2018911922

Print information available on the last page.

This book is printed on acid-free paper.

Scripture quotations marked NKJV are taken from the New King James Version. Copyright © 1982 by Thomas Nelson, Inc. Used by permission. All rights reserved.

Photo by Bob Valdez

DEDICATION

To my son, KD, my hero, chef, and my precious gift.

To my friends, who bless my life with love and laughter.

To all my family, who are lovely, rare, and great class rooms.

May these words, which I value as golden, be a clarion call
to grow forward to higher, holier passageways of thought,
and a flourishing, deeply intimate relationship with God.

APPRECIATION

Thank You, God!

Thank You for directing me to journal, constantly downloading Your sparkling truths and revelations of the uncommon, the unknown, and the misunderstood, AKA turning the light on!

For Your many outrageous expressions of love, unspeakably overwhelming trust, and unimaginable plans, I am grateful.

I appreciate the many countless number of teachers, mentors, leaders, friends, family, encouragers, prayers, challenges, difficulties, wonderful and not-at-all-wonderful things, peoples, and mentalities. En masse, whether knowingly or unknowingly, they have assisted the learning of what I didn't know but needed to know, and confirmed what I did know but didn't know I knew! It's grace, which is forever undeserved, and always, always amazing. I remain in awe!

I am more than grateful to share what is dear to my heart, and what I am yet learning.

COMMENTS & ENCOURAGEMENTS

Ivory Stone has written a must read for every Christian who wants to live life by design and not by default.

Her strong faith in God, for several decades, brings her experience and wisdom that will change and challenge every reader. It is a privilege to call her friend.

Tim Storey ~ Life Coach ~ Author
Pastor, The Congregation Church ~ Placentia, CA

We love *Sometimes, Some People & Some Thoughts*! It's as if God has given words from the Throne Room just for us! It so challenged and convicted us. We cried and laughed out loud.

What a great reminder of who we are in Christ, and Who He is within us. We've been refreshed in our souls and spirits, compelled by its instruction, and we're stirred to do more.

Thank you for sharing wisdom and encouragement to walk in faith much deeper. This book will be a blessing to many!

Mando & Arline Gonzales ~ Pastors & Leaders
Victory Outreach ~ Chino, CA

When you read the God ordained words contained in this book, it becomes clear, Ivory Stone sees from a higher place. Having known her for over 25 years, her amazing insights and revelations from God leave me desiring to reach for a pen and paper!

In my work as a counselor to Military Families, sometimes my own heart needs a chaplain. Ivory tops my trusted, spiritual advisor list. So grab a cup of coffee, and get ready for some mind-blowing inspiration, straight from the heart of God!

Cindy Hurd ~ LCSW-C
Brunswick, MD

This devotional is a must for anyone with a dream, and struggling to keep it going. Ivory Stone is truthful, honestly writing about some of the uglier realities that come up when you're in pursuit of your dreams.

The book encourages you to push past jealousy, fear, stress, and worry. Each 'Day' is filled with Scriptures to keep you moving forward. It's a help to level the playing field, like having a cheer leader in your corner, assuring you that God is with you!

Lexi Grace ~ Comedienne/Filmmaker
Toluca Lake, CA

Reading this book will remind you to become a student of the the Word of God. Perusing its encouragement, day after day, you're reminded that trials and negative circumstances are un-avoidable, but God shows up with victory!

It's most important to discover God loves us unconditionally, no matter our mistakes or faults. In that reality, we grow to under-stand the person of who we are, and our significance to God.

Mrs. Wallie Martin ~ Altadena, CA

For many years, I've taken classes, attended churches and religious events. My thoughts concerning religion told me God was an abstract - a far away ideology, and almost impossible for me to grasp and hold onto.

But after reading these pages, I now *know* that I am God's child, created in His image, and my relationship with God is not optional, or an illusion, but my reality! 'Sight is in the eye, but vision is in the heart' is part of my daily declaration.

I love the way the writer presents the information. She makes a practical application of spiritual truths and principles, which has caused me to get a hold of God, my Father!

Helen B. Carpenter ~ Monrovia, CA

FOREWORD

Feeling the urge and unction to write another book, I thought I'd first review the many journals stock piled in my office, car, bedroom, bookcases, and secret places. That led me to find voluminous mountains of notes, some falling from the various journals, and to place them in several stacks on my desk.

After sorting, dating and collating, amazed by the crazy number of journals and loads of notes, I was stunned to have so much spiritual fabric. Then, as only God can be stunning-er, I was speechlessly undone when I randomly picked up a note from a stack and read: "*God says, 'Write all the words I have spoken to you in a book.' Jeremiah 30:2"*. Uh, okay!

Frozen, hands shaking, eyes stuck, clutching my pearls, all I could do was 'Whew' a lot, with lots of tears. I cried, "O God!", a lot, as well. In that moment of wonder, in my personal and office disarray, there was a holy stillness. It continued, lingering. It was within me, on me, and around the room. It was a calming peace and a fiery excitement at the same time. In that moment, I sensed a lean-in from Heaven. For certain, and for me, it was a *God is here with you, right now,* experience!

There are no special effects or words that adequately describe God showing up. It's an inexplicable! First of all, it's not like an appointment you schedule. He's everywhere at the same time, all the time. But the 'lean-in' part is all His idea. Usually, it's a phenomenal unexpected. Yes, for sure, we can sense God in church, prayer times, moments of crises or great joy. But when you're doing life, or nothing at all or anything of note, nor tending to some 'holy' task, He can God on you!

Needful to say, it's a rich goodness, coolness, and beautifulness in your face! It makes you 'still' to know He is SO God! And you never get used to it. Each encounter is uniquely off the chart amazing, life changing, intimate, and very sweet!

After composing myself enough to realize an assignment had been given and was 'on', I paced and praised for quite a few days. It's my way of taking it all in, questioning my own ability to do the task, figuring out details, formats, and so on. Within my heart, however, I had a knowing that if God did speak on the randomly selected note, He's got a plan for accomplishing The Assignment. I get to be His accomplice!

Daily, I purpose, I try, to relinquish my rights to worry, stress or fear. Sometimes, it's not easy. Some people can truly confirm that. Some thoughts in my head, good and bad, could have influenced me to sway. But my decided focus on the office moment was the yielding God used to urge me in the surpassing reality and my reasoning direction for His will to be done.

Whether we write books, birth babies or projects, bear up under brutish situations, breakdance or bake pies, focus is a discipline required to produce well. It's a decision God blesses with great consequential returns. It's not our cleverness, talent, grit, labor or tenacity alone. It takes all that, settled on a combo plate of yielding to God and His sanctions for our good, and for our good success. Our 'lean-in' to God is the valve to His go, His yes, His green light, His show up and show off!

Pondering the note-taking, the journals, the years of hope-to-be-shared wisdoms, the evolving, God voiced statements, I'm finding greater relevance and application now than earlier on. Like an aged wine, or a better-the-next day sauce, the fullest measure gets assigned to 'the' appointed time. It's in growing, a vital part of the preparation process, we receive what's been purposed and ordained in full. The wait can be great, as in so cool, when focus isn't on the timing, but on the accomplishing.

Sometimes it's hard. Then there's some people who may influence or affect. Some thoughts can provoke or prompt change. Over and over, again and again, the *sometimes*, *some people*, and *some thoughts* continually halogenly lit my mind. I found: situations can be teachable 'sometimes'; we're ALL 'some people' at points in our life; 'some thoughts' that differentiate and stir the soul are helpful. Ah, revelation, and a title! Who knew? It wasn't pizza! It *was* a word and another lean in from God!

God *will* lean into your life and scenarios! You can be certain: He Who began a good work in you will complete it (Philippians 1:6). It was when you had no place on earth, having not been born, that God leaned in, with His creative genius, to make a plan, full of great ideas, *just for you*! He waited for the set, appointed time, the appropriate moment, to show up in your personal, assigned space. He came to breathe out purpose and accelerate a predestinated agenda, in which you star.

The urging that pushed me into my office, to the journals and stacks of notes, was God. His promptings provoke us to move, to do more, to leave where we have been, in order to arrive at a 'where' we've not been, seen or thought of before. His cleverness is wrapped with extremely loving Fatherness, as only He can give as our ultimate Parent, and as God Almighty!

I delight in God for the privilege of penning what I'm learning, what I received, heard, read, and am recalling from His revelations, sincerely valuing the diverse vehicles of their delivery. 'Wow' profusely falls from my lips, and on a regular basis!

Every whosoever, whose eyes take in these pages, is a grace upon this privileged grace! By faith, I declare the words herein will connect to their spirit, affect their lives, and be a deep well of encouragement. I thank God for being His child, and for gifting me to become His accomplice to this accomplishment!

MISSIVE

The intention of this journal is to turn up your volume of love, pursuit, and passion for God. Each day's light reveals facets and glimpses, revelations and aspects of the God of this faith walk, with journey factors not always taught or discussed, nor often considered. The contemporary language used is to override any religious overtones that may prevent a pure, from the heart expectation to encounter and to connect with God.

Following the path of genuine pursuit results in finding more of the Pursued, God - Father, Son, and Holy Spirit, and Their attributes and relevance to our lives. God promises to reward us for seeking Him (Hebrews 11:6). The prize is *having* more God than we imagined possible. Attached is the bonus of discovering more truth about our not-too-well known identity, purpose, liberty, and mostly unknown significance to God.

The daily format guides the way. Add you, your faith, your prayers, your desire for God, and your own personal energy. Allow this journal to be your coach. Be open to God's lavish love for you. Reach out to access His graces, truth, power, peace, and so many other benefits - all available and gifted to you!

Fearlessly, by faith, take courage to receive and know more of God Almighty, yourself, and what He has in store just for you!

EN ROUTE

1. The *Sometimes, Some People & Some Thoughts* in life, come our way to frame our world with wisdom and insight that may be unfamiliar to our way of thinking, and unknown to our usuals. A great way to assimilate new knowledge and information is to observe it objectively, rather than subjectively, without judgment, opinion or criticism. It's a selfless way to utilize what can be a catalyst of significant change. If we do so, and well, we are better able to absorb the whole truth, employing fresh perspicacity, and the revelatory support that truth presents.

2. When unencumbered by externals, the heart of man yields to its innate proclivity to reach for higher, greater levels of existence. This inner yearning turns us toward our Creator, from Whom we receive the sustenance He alone can supply. In His love, He hastens His response to graciously bestow gratifying fulfillment of our hunger and thirst, and our desire for Him.

3. BE READY. . . prepared, malleable, and open to receive.

BE SET. . . focused on forward, higher, and beyond.

GROW ON. . . past what was and all the priors, to an untrodden, predestined and fabulous future. It's right in front of you, with your name on it, awaiting your acceptance. Let it be seen in and on you. Now is the time, and it is <u>your</u> time!

1ST

QUARTER

DAY 1

GOD Is Always Almighty! He Is Never Almost.

This is the day that the LORD has made!
We will rejoice and be glad in it.
Psalm 118: 24

PRAYER: Father, I thank You for right now,
for trusting me with a fresh, new day! Lord,
thank You for giving me life and Your every
sufficiency to live and enjoy this gift. Please
lead and guide my steps, keeping me in my
lane, with the strength and wisdom to walk
well, straight, forward, and toward You.

Lord, thank You for favor and protection, for
good success and health. I thank You, God,
for loving me, for blessing me with You, and
for never underwhelming me! In the name
of Jesus, I pray and believe. . .

SOMETIMES. . . we dream! What's so amazing is there's power within God-given dreams. Like seeds of destiny, inside them is provision, promise, protection, possibility, and great purpose to reach far beyond anyone's personal or individual imaginings, or any singular interpretation.

God seals Himself in and on your dreams because they are from Him, and are expressions of Who He is. As well, they're a part of who you are, a measure of you that rises above the haltings of your environmental conditions and experiential barometers. Yet, both elements mesh declaring you quite able to labor them to birth, and nurture them to life.

Dreams cause your soul's mind, will and emotions to deeply drink from your spirit, your heart, the very core of your being. From that place, they draw out divine creativity. What gets released is a force, a power and grace, full of revelation, that offsets every natural sway to lesser places of influence.

It is the God of your dreams Who keeps you, refreshing your page within, until the dream emerges. This same loving God will make you lie down in green pastures of restoration, giving you the strength and presence of mind to follow Him in paths of excellence, and the extraordinary. These acts are His giftings which set you and your dreams apart from mediocrity.

Every make-a-difference dream will face opposers, challengers, doubters, and haters. If there are none of these, nor parasitic distracters, question whether it is God-given or you-driven. When a dream is non-threatening to the kingdoms of darkness and worldliness, or average and ordinary, it may be suspect. Examine its ability to carry enough depth of substance.

In the process of dreams coming true, there are roads divinely ordained that you don't get to build, nor necessarily like. But the terrain must be traversed to assure proper developmental progression. The turns, climbs, the pulls, pains, the ugly cries with deep sighs are the birth pangs of what has not been seen or done, nor thought of or born before.

Fulfillment includes disappointment, great labor, uncertainty, and, of course, stress. These markers, by God's design, deepen your perceptions and grow you in experiential knowledge. Appreciation and gratitude will begin to swell as you become an accomplice to a great accomplishment. The contrary is a stumbling out of purpose into a dreamless slumber of ease.

Listen for God to speak destiny to your dreams. They are His reality for you, but totally unattainable by you alone. For He imparts dreams that are somewhat consistent with the desires of your heart, which He strategically crafts into every fiber of your being, and onto the path of your purpose.

A dream, then, is a desire by design much bigger than you, and beyond where you are right now. But inside the dream is a picture of you not seen by you just yet. As the picture comes into focus, you will begin to see through it to much more, and past just you. With eyes wide open, you will begin to influence your future, affecting the expanse of your reach to everything, everyone, and every work of your hands.

The manifestation of your dream is a tapestry intricately woven with promise, and divinely downloaded to you when God caused you to dream. The promise is a prophecy forth-telling of its success, its importance to and impact on all who experience its reality of truth, creativity and effect.

Your dreams are key to the future God planned, destined, and called you to. You have been chosen to dream dreams, like Joseph did (Genesis 37-50), that will touch generations.

Dreams are waiting for you to awaken to them, to see and experience their manifestations more brilliant than technicolor! You alone must shake them to life. Only you can stir them to fullness, keeping them pure, relevant, and vibrantly alive.

Always deliberately dream big! Always remember God, your Dream Giver, is quite able to do exceedingly and abundantly above all you could hope, ask, think, imagine, or dream!

SOME PEOPLE. . . read more make believe and fantasy in novels than they pursue truth. Others watch television like it's a lover, focus on social media, or their neighbor's car, but are blind to life's realities. Many rally to protect wild life while they tearlessly abuse or abort their own children.

There are folk who fight for their rights to be wrong but, at the same time, they avoid considering anyone else's rights. As a custom, they opt to completely ignore decency and order.

But wisdom's eyes have right vision which not only sees what is happening in truth, but what could happen, and what should be happening. Vision deposits pictures in the mind and in the heart, causing hope to rise up above 'what is', to found what can, should, and shall be - clearly new ways to life and living.

Psalm 37:30 The mouth of the righteous utters wisdom, and
his tongue speaks with justice.
Psalm 111:10 The fear of the Lord is the beginning of wisdom;
all those who practice it have a good understanding.
Proverbs 24:3-4 Through wisdom a house is built, and by understanding it is established; by knowledge the rooms are
filled with all precious and pleasant riches.
James 1:5 If any of you lacks wisdom, let him ask of God,
Who gives to all liberally and without reproach,
and it will be given to him.

SOME THOUGHTS. . .

FACE TIME God! Get up close and personal in your pursuit
of Him, for His face is always and forever toward you.

One good thing about a storm - it allows us to realize, know,
and acknowledge our actual need for God.
A storm can escort us into a relationship with God which we
wouldn't have otherwise encountered without it.
Thank God for the storm that brought you to Him which was,
unbeknownst to you, a result of His relentless pursuit of you.
Why? It's simply because He loves you madly!

Consider forgiveness - a move forward, wearing new clothes!
It is fresh garments making you look much better than the outdated clothes of past hurts and foul feelings of insignificance,
tainted with tear stains from vile violations.
It is a walk past all that with the swag of a new liberty to move
in a free, higher, greater dimension of you!

God is really good at using methods that look like madness.
How good are you at trust?

The most fragrant flower in the garden of life is gratitude.

I DECLARE. . . Today I will walk in the power and protection of God Who loves me. Therefore, I will not walk in fear.

PSALM 107:43 ~ If you are really wise, you'll think this over — it's time you appreciated God's deep love (for you!).

NOTES & OBSERVATIONS. . .

_____

_____

_____

_____

_____

_____

_____

_____

_____

_____

_____

_____

_____

_____

_____

_____

_____

DAY 2

*GOD Is Able To Restore Your Soul's Peace,
And Your Mind's Power.*

Fear not, for I have redeemed you. I have
called you by your name. You are Mine!

Isaiah 43:1b

PRAYER: O Redeemer, how can I thank You?
You have called me out of darkness into Your
marvelous light. Father, I am grateful that You
accept me as Your own child, keeping me full
in the provision and protection of Your care in
all matters, and every day of my life.

Lord, teach me how to expect You daily! Make
my ears sensitive to hear and know Your voice
above my own, and all others. O God, help me!
Impart to me Your grace to become all that You
created and expect me to be. I give my thanks
to You, Lord, in Jesus' name. . .

SOMETIMES. . . we get stuck! Stuck - as in the place we stay way too long. Paralyzed, atrophied, we're frozen by disappointments, heartaches, headaches, fall downs, and setbacks. We could call them blockages, or maybe consequences, from our choices that made those 'Uh oh!?' moments. We're stuck, avoiding the changes needed to make a move on. We're on, but on stuck, because we can't get past where we are.

Satisfaction can come easy in stuck places. There's no desire nor demand for better, for new, or for more. We may seek bits of comfort because, in the fray of stuck, we grow weary from thoughts of pushing past objections to moving forward. Plus, it's hard dealing with the emotions of our long ago thens, and way back whens which linger, longing to become the filter of our nows' realities. These possessive captors keep us caught, on lockdown, unable to think right or believe for different.

Problems peak when our stuck mentality keeps God stuck outside of our immobility. The probability of morphing into who He made us to be is recklessly abandoned. We begin serving God from memory rather than from intention, or love and desire for Him. We're too pained to pursue in the stuck place.

Case in point, when Israel cried for freedom in their Egyptian bondage and it was time to go, they did not *want to* because

Egypt was their *secure place* (Exodus, chapters 6-12). They denied God being their true security by clinging to Egypt. Israel liked the familiar security of their personal prison of stuck. We, like Israel was with Egypt, prefer the familiarity of routine to accompany our captivity. The mix of solely surviving with a regimen of no real personal responsibility is faintly tart-sweet.

In the stayed position, many stuck-ees opt to recoil from personal responsibility. In essence, they choose to be miserably meager in their semi-security rather than to be fully secure in their freedom. They don't understand doing nothing is more depleting and exhausting than expending energy on effort.

What they, and we, get used to doing in the stuck place will supersede their actual ability, their 'can do', their much required 'want to', to develop their desire for better. Lulled to sleep, we all nap in order to forget God created us to function with a far greater capacity, and on a much higher level of awake!

Unfortunately, comfort, convenience and ease, at a minimum, can seduce us to surrender our pursuit and appreciation of the beautiful place of better. Alas, we settle. We choose a kinda, sorta comfort and ease, over the Comforter and pleasing God. We're stuck in mediocrity, a semi-comfort zone, AKA a C.Z. In truth, no matter how big a C.Z. (cubic zirconia, or artificial diamond) may be, it's still a fake. It's pretty, but not precious.

Stuck-ness deceives. It feeds us its bait of dispassion. We get consumed, confounded and conned by our current conditions, scary scenarios, and raw realities. Since stuck is a stagnancy, we're numbed into having no mindful motivation or impulse to move. It is a colorless, empty room. Much like a frustrating occupation, or a jail sentence, it's devoid of benefits, or the possibility of parole. Forget about that corner office with a window and a view, or a cool cell mate. We're swayed away, far from woke, without ever recognizing we are free to go!

God never called us to be better slaves! But He did call us out of darkness into His marvelous light (1 Peter 2:9). A stuck locale is a room with no light. It's dark in there! We must stay in the light to recognize and avoid luring leftovers from the past.

What's scary true is darkness, another name for ignorance, is where the enemy operates by taking advantage of what we do not know. If we don't know God that well, it can become a big, fat playground for more stuck-nesses, lures, and lockdowns.

But God has plans for our specific needs and, *if* we are willing to be loosed, a way of escape! In that stuck, dark, empty place, the first help we need is detachment, a let-it-go release to freedom. The next help is remembering *who we are*, a child of God, chosen, called, free, lit, and made to be *stayed* in the beauty of all that to move, unglued, freed and forward!

SOME PEOPLE. . . never listen to understand what they're hearing. They listen for their opportunity to reply.

Proverbs 1:5 A wise man will hear and increase learning, and a man of understanding will attain wise counsel.

SOME PEOPLE. . . harbor angst against other folk for a lifetime over something that occurred in a moment of time.

Proverbs 16:32 He who is slow to anger is better than the mighty, and he who rules his spirit is better than he who takes a city.

Matthew 7:1-2 Don't pick on people, jump on their failures, criticize their faults — unless, of course, you want the same treatment. That critical spirit has a way of boomeranging.

SOME PEOPLE. . . want to know stuff to help other folk know stuff, while some people want to know stuff just so other folk know that they know stuff.

Proverbs 2:6 All wisdom comes from the Lord, and so do common sense and understanding.

Acts 20:35 It's more blessed to give than to receive.

SOME THOUGHTS. . .

When a close friend agrees to do something, and gives their word, it would be an insult to say, 'I sure hope you will'.

You might go there if it's someone you just met, or it's merely an acquaintance. Such doubt is unbefitting a real close friend. How much more should we trust God Who has an impeccable reputation for doing what He says, and Who *is* Truth? God will never prank us or dangle carrots, nor is He careless with us. His integrity and character immensely excel that of all others.

Proverbs 3:5-6 Lean on, trust in, and *be confident* in the LORD with all your heart, and do not rely on your own understanding. In all your ways acknowledge Him, and He will direct and
make straight and plain your paths.

Bonding with the wrong people or cause produces bondage.

God's will is His expressed desire and mindful plan for us. It is never His demand. But it is our choice to always choose wisely!

Never regret getting older. Just make sure you're growing in that getting. Besides, it's a privilege not everyone receives.
That's because anybody can be young.

I DECLARE. . . I am a child of God, made in His image,
with His signature on my soul.

EPHESIANS 1:5 ~ He predestined us for adoption to Himself as
sons through Jesus Christ, according to the purpose of His will.

NOTES & OBSERVATIONS. . .

_____

_____

_____

_____

_____

_____

_____

_____

_____

_____

_____

_____

_____

DAY 3

GOD's Word Is Never Without Power,
Because It Is Himself.

You are the light of the world. Let your light
so shine before men, that they may
see your good works and glorify
your Father in heaven.
Matthew 5:14a, 16

PRAYER: God, thank You for crafting plans
to establish my goings, my efforts, my work,
and my life. Lord, direct me to walk boldly in
the way that aligns with Your purpose.

Father, show me who I can touch today with
You. Fill me with Your Word, Your light, and
Your love for others. Use me to give You to
those who don't know You yet. Make me a
blessing to someone for Your sake. Please
make the fruit of my lips a great praise and
thanks to You, in Jesus' name. . .

SOMETIMES. . . we get a dam problem! A dam is built to form a barrier to control the flow of water. This applies to life in both the natural and in the spiritual realms. In reality, we choose to build up our dam problem by constructing barriers that dam up the flow of what we need for a God life.

Our problem is the dam problem keeps God from flowing out to reach us with His Living Water. When that occurs, we dry up. We're in drought, which can lead to famine since our dam problem blocks God's provision and supply, the needed grace elements of His Living Water, from irrigating the arid, indigent places in our soul, and enabling function in our lives.

When we forget who we are - a child of God, and Whose we are - His, we must become as the Prodigal and return to our senses (Luke 15:17). Why allow the stresses and anxiety of dam problems to keep us drained by them, and from Him?

In our dry, parched state of mind, we forgo relying on God's Fatherness and sufficiency. We thirst after this truth: Be still, and know that I am God (Psalm 46:10a). God, the Builder, is our Father! We're under construction and His instruction.

It's great to be grown, but it's greater to be God's own child, soaking in His presence, fluid with His abundance, following His way for us, to avoid those unnecessary dam problems!

SOME PEOPLE. . . become friends and family with their conditions of life because they have no desire to change. Perhaps they're afraid of change, or are unwilling to spy out a different direction. 'Why fix what ain't broke?' is commonly interjected whenever the confrontation of truth shows up.

And the answer is: Addiction isn't always drug related. Mentalities that tether folk to what they have in mind, or to their way of doing things, can be strongholds just as addictions can be. Like tattoos, strongholds are engraved, but on the soul, a not so easily erased canvas. The challenge to undo and unlearn is great due to being birthed in a 'what I want' behavior.

To grow into change is to be in a state of avail to turning the page and changing the channel. It's being teachable, open to discovering new. A 'this only' mindset is a growth inhibiter and a life limiter, not to mention grey, dull, and boring.

The idea of being God's child speaks to our dependency on, trust in, and followship of His plan, will and purpose. When He leads us, in every state and all stages of our existence, we get loosed from the old of ordinary. It's a matter of us choosing to lay down our resistance and consternation over change. It's a little awkward, but so is walking in new shoes. Even if we are infected with misoneism, we can be healed, in Jesus' name! Besides, *ONLY* God changes not (Malachi 3:6).

SOME THOUGHTS. . .

Never accept a piece of peace.
Peace is never trying to please, ease, grease or appease any-
      one. It's never a go-along-to-get-along mindset.

Peace is from Jesus, the Lord, Who is the Prince of Peace.
At its core is willingness to resolve conflict without compromise.

Peace is pure power and real, genuine righteousness.
Its voice can be still, or a silent roar, sounding its strength,
      calm certainty, and rule in the places it dwells.

Every blessing God has for us requires something from us.
Begin with faith and prayer. Add obedience. Plant copious
seeds of generosity. Temper every effort with giving thanks,
praise, and honor. Then, rest your faith in Him, trusting
      wholly, doubtlessly, in His faithfulness.

The more we abide in the Word of God, the more sensitivity
we will have to truth. The result is a developed instinct
      to know what is and what is not of God.

How well you rest in God is determined by how well you walk
      in faith, in love, and complete trust in God.

I DECLARE. . . Today I will experience God's favor in new ways! I am grateful for new doors of supernatural opportunity.

PSALM 16:8 ~ I keep my eyes always on the LORD. With Him at my right hand, I will not be shaken.

NOTES & OBSERVATIONS. . .

DAY 4

GOD Sees Us, Knows Us, And Loves Us Still!

I am like a flourishing olive tree in the
house of God. I trust in His constant
love forever and ever.
Psalm 52:8

PRAYER: Father, Your love is precious to
me. I can scarcely imagine it's mine. Lord,
I thank You for every gesture of generosity
You give me unconditionally, just because
You love me. God, Your love is more than
amazing, and it is forever!

Please give me the grace to love like You,
to forgive as You do. Give me the wisdom,
the courage, and the desire to be like You
in my life, in what I do, and in my spheres
of influence. God, thank You for receiving
my heart's gratitude, in Jesus' name. . .

SOMETIMES. . . we're guilty of crimes against ourselves. We may be guilty of contributing to situations that caused our pain, frustration, shame, and tremendous emotional ructions. The residue remains, disrupting life and robbing our peace.

We've got to examine exactly what we did, despite the dreaded unpleasantries of revisiting memories we'd like buried. As brutal as it is, we must consider the possibility of having been a perpetrator of our own victimization. For sure, there are the outside factors to check, but we can't lessen the significance of the inside elements. Sherlock Holmes wouldn't!

Closure and healing will show up big when our effort to take ownership and responsibility, for what we did or did not do, is placed face up on the table. Thoroughly inspecting ourselves, fully assessing our participation and motives, judging rightly, may cause tears and answers to flow into the mending.

The problem is, when we're hurting or feel shame, we blame. It's an automatic go to, a refugee hiding place behind the faults of others. But in truth, it's accusation and excuse to devise a conveniently comfortable coverup for our unhealed wounds.

The solution, a balm of recovery, is looking, #1. To see inside ourselves, and #2. To know the why behind making our wrong, weak, not-so-wise choices in the first place. This is especially necessary when problematic situations tend to draw out patterns of unconscious, habitual behavior. Our automatics then develop into weapons of mass self-destruction. It's like giving bullets to the one - you, shooting at you. YIKES!

Boundaries work well, not only for those we're in relationship or associated with, but they help to personally protect us from us. They are a restraining order we issue - a note to self, to keep our old dysfunctionalities from returning to intimidate, harass, abuse, or beat up the 'who' we are becoming.

While drawing up those boundary schematics, we would do well to trust 1 John 1:9's text: IF we confess our sins, God is faithful and just to forgive us our sins, and *cleanse us from all* unrighteousness. It means He will *also* wash away the effects of sin imposed on us by other folk (SWEET!). No more blame, guilt, or shame! Why keep reviewing, rehearsing, and holding onto what God has forgiven, unfriended, and forgotten?

If we choose to agree with God, He'll arrange the change. It can happen *if* we decide to STOP in the name of the love He has for us, the love we should have for ourselves, and for all those we used to blame. We can do this, people! Philippians 4:13 is huge: 'I *can* do all things through Christ Who strengthens me.' O thank God for His very cool Cleanser-ness!

SOME PEOPLE. . . stop giving in fear that those they give to may surpass them in some way.

Luke 6:38 Give, and *it will be given to you*: good measure, pressed down, shaken together, and running over, will be put into your bosom. For with the same measure that you use, it will be measured back to you. Give BIG!

SOME PEOPLE. . . are religious, kinda like the Pharisees.

They are never happy unless they are right, which means they are only happy if you are wrong.

God calls us to relationship, righteousness, peace, and love. He never mentioned I'm-always-right-ness.

SOME PEOPLE. . . mask their fears and veil their issues by shrouding them behind anger, impatience, insensitivity, bad behavior, aggression, isolation, and other quagmired hot messes.

They forgot, or never learned, God loves us with a perfect love that casts out fear (1 John 4:18), and heals what we stop hiding. Jesus' Cross set us free from every captivity, making us able to receive His graces in full, openly and fearlessly!

2 Timothy 1:7 For God has not given us a spirit of fear, but of power, of love, and of a sound mind (self control).

SOME THOUGHTS. . .

Prayer is being open and vulnerable before God, the Father
Who will not shame or take advantage of us.

Genuine gratitude grows into deeper appreciation.

Whatever preoccupies you from your purpose is a squatter
on your assignment in need of eviction.

To qualify to obtain, we must develop the capacity to maintain
what we qualify for. Simply steward wisely.

Offense can cause physical impairment because it's a weighty
load in your soul, much too heavy to carry.

Faith is a decision *to believe* God is, *to accept* the sovereignty
of His will in doing what He does, *to know* His Word is enough,
and *to accept* it as God, Who can be trusted.

When uneasiness overshadows a situation, a person, a place
or a thing, it may be a Holy Ghost flag on the field. Stay woke!

I DECLARE. . . I know God loves me with an always and
forever, unconditional and everlasting love.

JOHN 14:1 ~ Do not let your hearts be troubled. Trust in
God, trust also in Me (Jesus).

NOTES & OBSERVATIONS. . .

_____

_____

_____

_____

_____

_____

_____

_____

_____

_____

_____

_____

_____

_____

DAY 5

GoD Already Forgave, And He's Ready To Save.

For whom He foreknew, He also predestined to be conformed to the image of His Son, that He might be the firstborn among many brethren.
Romans 8:29

PRAYER: Dear Lord, You are my Father and the Rescuer of my life. You drew me out from great danger into the light of Your love! Thank You for saving me and my future from my past and myself, and from every destruction.

Father, call me closer to You. Stay me always before You. Help me see and know more than my eyes and my mind can see and know. I set my face as a flint toward You! Fix my focus on You, Lord. Help my mind remain on You and in Your peace. I thank You for loving me, for Your every kindness, and for blessing my heart. It is in the name of Jesus, my Savior, I pray. . .

SOMETIMES. . . we struggle reconfiguring plans to grow forward. It's a challenge to deal with the process of transition. The transition between what we were, what we are now, and what we are to be and do is hard. More stress may show up over who we are now and who we are to become.

The struggle surfaces because many of us do not know *who* we are. We get caught up in what we do, what we did, and what we have. All these 'whats' confuse us. According to our culture, critics, the world and us, we're subject to be judged and audited by our accomplishments and acquisitions. If the real truth be told, 'who' we are has zero to do with that.

Another fun fact is lots of people tag themselves according to where they came from, what they did, and what histories they happened through. We may have attached ourselves to phenomenal defining moments, both positive and negative, but none of them define the 'who' of who we truly are.

As Believers, before we are male, female, black, brown, blue, red, doctor, lawyer, dancer, astronaut, brilliant, short, deaf, or a whosoever, we are <u>first</u> His, as in God's child. Innocently or ignorantly, fearfully or defiantly, we seldom live our lives predicated on this enormous position of power and criteria of identity. Since many of us struggle with our true 'who', it is no mystery why we're uncomfortable sitting in the chair of change.

How do we transition out from so lesser a degree of thought to an unimaginable mindset, far beyond our pay scale? It's Joseph becoming a prince straight out of prison!

Every human ever born has been crafted by God, the Creator, and given purpose, the real reason for being born. God has designs on us. His signature is on our soul. But without an encounter with this great God, we can't know Him or His plans and intentions for us, nor can we know who we are.

By His benevolent strategies and skill treasuries, God works all things out for our good. Life's storms, enigmas, and not-so-fun insurmountables are tooled to scooch us closer and closer to Him while we're on safari for the answers to 'why'. It's a setup for us to become the captured hunter! We get caught by a waiting God longing to pour on us His love and Daddy-ness, and inform us of His plans for a life we know not of.

As our responses to God become more 'yes-ing', and our actions more yielding, the struggle of change, especially into a King's Kid ID, fades. By His grace, we discover the eternal truth - we are chosen, called, set apart, and so loved by God Almighty! Little by little, we morph into *who* we are. It may be hard, yea awkward, to believe God really likes us that much. But our yes-ing and yielding, His gracing and loving, are the fashioning tools that never fail to change hearts and lives!

SOME PEOPLE . . . get corrected and redirected, but still find it difficult to grasp the liberating power of repentance. It's usually because they have a 'want to' contrary to the 'want to' God has in mind for their lives. They're kinda, maybe without realizing it, courting rebellion, a pushback from grace.

The same folk 'want to' receive immediate responses to their prayer requests, but have trouble making good efforts to respond as fast to God's ideologies. They probably jes' forgot He did call it what is it, sin, which has not-at-all profitable side effects. And another problem sin creates, it cumbers communication with God. He's not deaf, but He won't *hear to respond* to their supplications for His stuff. He does answer mercifully, with all deliberate quietude, as in crickets!

On the other hand, when correction is received, it is cathartic to the once wayward soul. It begins, like surgery, to cut away the error and sin, the toxic deceptions and carcinogens. It neutralizes, by its conviction, poisonous contraries, layered in the atmosphere of misaligned mindsets and unwise choices, subtly produced by the enemy, and yes-ed by the flesh.

Now, more than ever, God is calling us to attention and order, to turn away from self and return to Him. Repent! The word means *to return to the top*, to God, to the lofty places of outrageous victory, the likes of which we've never imagined.

Repentance is a change of mind to realign with God. It is an out loud declaration of dependence on Him, and a radical expression of surrender to God, which can be wildly contagious. It's a confession of agreement with His will and plans to bless us His way, an always-so-much-more way than our own.

God gifts us repentance, a not used enough grace, a get back on track to the top, where He's found and waiting. It is not a screaming and crying, falling out in the floor and shaming ourselves session. Its profundity of intention holds a passionate intensity, reaching deeper and past any 'I'm sorry'.

Repentance brings about a complete heart and mind change with an organic amenity of new and improved behavior. It's a spiritual coming-to-our-senses sensibility which, as well, stirs our emotions to order. Tears may fall, but tears that cleanse and purge refresh the soul. Yes, ugly cries accepted.

Repentance is saying, 'God, I want back with You', though He and His love never left for a moment, and never will.

Psalm 51:10 Create in me a clean heart, O God, and renew
          a right spirit within me.
Proverbs 10:17 He who keeps instruction is in the way of life,
          but he who refuses correction goes astray.
2 Corinthians 7:10 For godly sorrow produces a repentance
          that leads to salvation without regret.

SOME THOUGHTS...

Trust in God is faith, dependency, and commitment to believe
He is always good, truthful, faithful, and loving.
It is relying completely on His strength, sovereignty, wisdom,
and track record without waiver, doubt or fear.

Once we are willing to let go of non-productive situations, or
people, we're able to clearly delineate between that that is
essential, and that that is distractive to purpose.

When one door closes, know that it must close before another
door to greater opportunity and possibility will open.
It's God's way to avoid any indecision, confusion, or clutter.

Enemies are another type of storm.
The blessing is they draw your focus to your need for God.

Money may temporarily resolve a reoccurring problem,
but only a mind change can eliminate it.

Great faith is developed in our response to God's silence.

I DECLARE. . . I stand in faith, believing to receive what God
has spoken to me, and I will not be disappointed!

2 SAMUEL 7:28 ~ O Sovereign LORD, You are God! Your
words are trustworthy, and You have promised
good things to Your servant.

NOTES & OBSERVATIONS. . .

_____

_____

_____

_____

_____

_____

_____

_____

_____

_____

_____

_____

DAY 6

GOD's Blessings Come With A Gift Of Grace To Enjoy Them.

Since we have a great High Priest Who has
ascended into heaven, Jesus, the Son of God,
let us hold fast to our confession.

Hebrews 4:14

PRAYER: My Father, I believe You! My faith is
in You. I believe You have a plan for my life that
is more than I deserve, and greater than I could
configure, imagine, or ever hope for.

O Lord, You said I am as the apple of Your eye!
Help me to live my life as that, pleasing You and
representing Who You are. Raise me up to Your
standard. I want to be one who honors You, one
who looks, thinks and acts like You, as Your own
child. Thank You for hearing me! Father, it is in
Jesus' amazing name, I pray. . .

SOMETIMES. . . God blesses people around us with what we actually and specifically had in mind for ourselves.

It can be so aggravating. We're provoked to jealousy, cringing and crying uncontrollably. While we kinda smile at them, we sorta say, 'Praise the Lord! Oh, that's so nice!'

Confusion adds to our emotional tilt, because it was what we were about to ask for! Fortunately, God is never our soul's tormentor. But, He is extremely clever at provoking us in order to create a need for Him, thus, getting us to dial Him up. Whether early in the AM, while the dew is still on the roses, or late in the midnight hour, God loves to hear us call His name.

God's provocation is a beautiful, well thought out plan. It's our wake up call out of our slumbering faith that holds us hostage to mediocrity, and settling for an 'it'll do' life. The revelation is seeing God as willing and well able to respond. It's the causal prompter to seek Him, and diligently, for all our answers, concerns, personal needs, and our unspoken heart desires.

1 Samuel 1:6 says that Peninnah, who had several sons and daughters, was a rival to Hannah, who was barren. Peninnah 'provoked her severely, to make her miserable'. It also *made* Hannah cry out to God, Who answered her with a son, Samuel the prophet, and five other children. That's SO nice!

Philippians 4:6 tells us: Be anxious for nothing, but in everything, by prayer and supplication, with thanksgiving, *let your requests be made known to God.* We've gotta ask, seek, and knock (Matthew 7:7) persistently, boldly, and confidently!

With that said, we can believe that 'no good thing will He withhold' from us when we stand in faith, trusting and seeking Him, our loving, gracious, O So Good Father (Psalm 84:11)!

SOMETIMES. . . a problem can be a gateway to your own recognition, recompense, acceptance, and significance.

Recalling the story of David and Goliath (I Samuel 17), had Mr. G not been on campus, Dave might have remained obscure in his identity, ill-acclaim, and sheep tending. Yes, he was anointed by God, but he had to do something to activate that oil.

Solving Israel's big, fat, 'giant' problem brought tremendous reward, celebrated value, and an amazing future to this young, underrated, unnoticed teenager. By making himself *available*, he made himself their answer.

Be courageous and avail yourself to God's Text Messages in the Bible. They will greaten your faith to follow His lead to your purpose and an exciting, wondrous journey to a vibrantly alive and abundant life. BE bold, BE ready, and BE God-fident!

SOME PEOPLE. . . avoid pursuit of relationship with God, and all the over the top, up close and personal stuff. The problem and fear for them is the more folk get to know Him, the more He reveals Himself and His ways. What that will do, as an added intrigue, is reveal more about them and their ways!

Even though it is wonderful God loves everybody, it might be a bit uncomfortable, and disconcerting, to hang out with Him. The challenge is bearing up under all that light and truth!

Another complication, once the door is open, He will close in, employing every effort to hold their attention and draw their affection. He won't leave them alone! He'll remain in hot pursuit, purposed to share His love and kindness, overflowing in every saving grace and mercy. Then comes His blatant blessings of provision, favor, and peace, making it definitely difficult to stand aloof from Him, turn away, or stay the same.

Because He's a really good and quite the faithful Friend, He'll message them through the voicings of their own friends who actually know Him. Adding fuel to the fire of His relentless outreach, these same friends keep testifying of His way coolness they've experienced first hand. Whosoever He's after should know His rep - He so loves them and won't forsake them! No one wise would resist or want a life outside all of this love, joy, radical fun, and rich relationship jes' waitin' for 'em!

SOME THOUGHTS. . .

Feed your mind to succeed in your life.
The mind needs nurturing, positive input, and right directives.

Aimed focus, resulting from proper perception and wise goal setting, is urgent to avoid constant replay of negatives, painful life events, factuals, untruths, and haunting historical issues.

Constructive instruction, to develop healthy mental habits and soul control, is required to further cause the mind to be servant and not master. Speaking life to it maximizes its functionality.

Teach your mind by way of pictures, examples, and positives. Harboring healthy thought patterns is a learned behavior which gets developed when practiced as a discipline.

The secret to mental strength and health is in absorbing God's Word, having clear, consistent, decisive self-talk, and fostering attitudes that project life, light, and truth. Your mind is the greatest of all your investments, and it is your power.

Give forgiveness to those who don't deserve it remembering always that God did it, and still does it, for you!

To avoid Hagar moments (Genesis 16), always wait on God!

I DECLARE. . . I commit to renew my mind daily by reading, believing, and confessing the Word of God.

ROMANS 12:2 ~ Do not be conformed to this world, but be transformed by the renewing of your mind, that you may prove what is that good and acceptable and perfect will of God.

NOTES & OBSERVATIONS. . .

_____

_____

_____

_____

_____

_____

_____

_____

_____

_____

_____

_____

_____

DAY 7

God Is Omnipotent! He Has No Rival.

Behold, God is my salvation, I will trust and
not be afraid, for the LORD is my strength
and song. He has become my salvation.

Isaiah 12:2

PRAYER: Dear God, please help me really
know You that I will know and recognize, for
certain, what is not You. Open my mind to an
understanding of Your ways in order to apply
them in my life, my thinking and my behavior,
so that I can affect the world around me.

Father, give me a passion to pursue You like
never before. Teach me to love You so that I
am pleasing to You. I give thanks for all Your
measures of grace You pour into my life. My
Lord, I will not take You for granted. My face
is toward You, in Jesus' name. . .

SOMETIMES. . . we *must* worship! It's spiritual breathing! Worship, aside from giving God our true self, takes us where our troubles can't find us. It is the gift of our attention and our heart to God which changes us, the worshiper.

True worship is birthed from recognizing God's worth, all that He is, and His immensely lavish love for us. It is the place we begin to know God in the joy of His person, not only as our Creator, but as our Father by kinship. In worship, we get to give God what He wants - *all* of us, withholding nothing.

Worship connects us in sweet intimacy with God by forging new depths and heights into our relationship with Him. His responses woo us, reaching the deepest places of the heart, even those broken, prompting the mends of change and release to Him within every part of us.

Sensing God's presence is disarming. It's an encounter drawing us into letting go - of us, what's inside us, and all else, to receive what we don't and can't have without Him. Sans this holy exchange, worship is incomplete. By this grace, we luxuriate in the throne room of His presence, changed by the saturation of His love and holiness, His refuge and safety.

When we worship, we talk with God, speaking a different language. It's a heart to heart conversation He waits to hear, for

He longs for the sound of our voice to bestir His Fatherness. We've got to worship, we must, to learn God loves us, desires us, knows us, and is responsible for us. We need to feel and know His eyes on us, in all our life processes, seeing and loving us in the grand or the raw, in our faith or doubt, or our fear.

Worship is a deeper place in God. It is more than a service at church, or a song's melody and rhyme. It's a sound that finds heaven, where God leans in, humbling Himself to consider us, to hear our concerns, and to attend our cries to Him.

Inside the heart of every man, woman and child, whether heathen, pagan, or Christian, is an innate need to reach for something greater than self. From Cain and Abel to Abraham and Isaac, Moses and Israel, Elijah and the prophets of Baal, worship was culturally a common practice, along with sacrifice. Both were integral parts of expressing personal beliefs.

Before the foundations of the earth were laid, before humanity knew to do so, God sacrificed Jesus, for He so loved us! This love should excite us to give our whole being back to Him in an almost febrile, fiery attitude of worshipful gratitude. It's due response to illimitable love! It's languaged emotion poured out of the depths of our soul. As David recommends: O Come, let us worship and bow down, let us kneel before the LORD, our Maker (Psalm 95:6). O Hallelujah, Amen!

SOME PEOPLE. . . know how to do church, however, they don't know how to do the Kingdom.

In truth, they haven't considered the Kingdom as the consolidation of all Jesus is, what He taught, and His way of doing things. The Kingdom is His righteousness, peace and joy, in the power of His Holy Spirit (Romans 14:17).

The Kingdom embodies His commission to go into the world, contagious with the knowledge of God, affecting people to get to know and follow Jesus. The Kingdom is Good News, AKA the Gospel, of God's crazy love and forgiveness, truth, hope, and abundant life. It comes with an invite to receive all these things, plus, a liberating, personal relationship with God.

To *only* do church is merely a religious exercise, which could also be compared to running on a treadmill. While a measure of success may be accomplished, such as weight loss, benefits are one dimensional - for a runner, who is in a room with a treadmill, but going absolutely nowhere. Selah!

SOME PEOPLE. . . forget it's not by cleverness, great abilities, mental astuteness, or talent, but by the power and grace of God's enablement *alone* that anyone is able to do anything.

SOME THOUGHTS. . .

When Noah built the ark, he had to believe in something he'd never seen before, something for which he had no point of reference. He had to believe, imagine forward and envision, like a dream, those things God had spoken and promised, though they were hidden in a future manifestation.

It was his faith that gave him the courage to believe God, and to expect Him to do the unthinkable, the unheard of, the inconceivable (Genesis 6:22, 7:5). And then, God did just that, every bit of it, like He said, and exactly as He promised!

Relationship is not something we 'get', like the acquisition of a new car, a raise, or a day at Disneyland. Much like faith, it's ever increasing, growing up and forward, and causing each of its involved partners to flourish because of it.

Whether a friend, a spouse, or God and you, both are fully vested, wholly involved, and completely committed to all the heart, beneficence, and beauty relationship is, offers, and gifts!

Never make an issue an idol.

Real worship is the greatest soul detox.

I Declare. . . I am a masterpiece, crafted by the hand of God. I display the creative genius of God Almighty, my Daddy!

John 14:27 ~ Peace I leave with you, My peace I give to you, not as the world gives do I give to you. Let not your heart be troubled, neither let it be afraid.

Notes & Observations. . .

_____

_____

_____

_____

_____

_____

_____

_____

_____

_____

_____

_____

_____

DAY 8

*GOD Will Not Fail You, Hurt You,
Abandon You, Forsake You, Or Shame You.*

For as high as the heavens are above the
earth, so great is His steadfast love
toward those who fear Him.

Psalm 103:11

PRAYER: O Lord, I'm so in awe of You!
I am amazed Your love for me is without
regard of my mistakes, faults, or failures.
You know me, and every thing about me,
all my heart's intent and content, and yet
You care about me, You're still with me!

Thank You, Lord, for never forsaking me,
for never leaving me alone. May I honor
You with my words and my thoughts, my
behavior and all my efforts because You
are my God, my only help and hope. It is
to You I give my thanks and praise, now
and always, in Jesus' name. . .

SOMETIMES. . . we go along to get along. We 'act' like we don't know what we do know to be accepted and to stay in the room with all the hater-ites, jealous-ites, intimidation-ites, and a number of those negative critter-ites.

But when we come *to know* who we really are - children of the only Living God, other folk, significant with purpose, will want to know us, who we are, Who we know, and what we know.

John 1:12-13 But as many as received Him, to them He gave *the right* to become children of God, to those who believe in His name: who were born, not of blood, nor of the will of the flesh, nor of the will of man, but of God.

SOMETIMES. . . it takes holding onto faith with everything inside you to believe that it should be *and will be* you who be- comes 'the first' in your family to have more than, and not just, a GED, but a college degree; 'the first' in your family to marry and have children, and stay married; 'the first' in your circle of friends who completely sidesteps the penitentiary of lack, lost identity, failure, dysfunction, and a bad history.

Jeremiah 29:11 "For I know the plans and thoughts that I have for you," says the LORD, "plans for peace and well-being and not for disaster, to give you a future and a hope."

SOME PEOPLE. . . are mild mannered, Clark Kent types. They are spiritual folk who don't quite understand the louder, wild and crazier, run around the room, shoutin' types.

The more reserved ones aren't like those fanatic ones at all. So not so! But they are those 'fans' who stand up screamin', shoutin', and yellin' to cheer on their team for that basket or the touchdown scored at the game! They would never think of themselves in anywise double-minded.

Considering the regularly loud, shoutin' folk, perhaps they do so because God made a miraculous slam dunk, or an unbe-lievable touchdown in their lives. Anyone would find it difficult to hold still and chill when some cancer left their body, or they got the job they weren't qualified for, or some big problem was suddenly solved. When a way out of no way shows up, erup-tions of loudly expressed gratitude are well warranted. Great responses to grace are seldom mere emotion running a room!

For sure, it's okay to be the quiet type. In fact, some encoun-ters with God will leave you speechless. It might be erudite to rethink the virtues of both the loud and the quiet.

For the case of the consistently clamorous, tolerance of their vociferousness should be given. After all, the Bible does say 'make a joyful noise' a few times! Many stories therein speak of people who got answers and miracles for crying out loudly, not whisperingly, to God. In 1 Samuel 1, Hannah was so loud and animated, Eli, the priest, said, "You're drunk!" Blind Bartimaeus' cries, in Mark 10, make him a premier example.

Note well, the more anyone gets to know God, not their clergy, church or denomination, the more they will desire to speak of Him, and very likely out loud! For the less louds, there's legitimacy for their stance in Habakkuk 2:20's Text: Let all the earth keep silence (in awe) before Him. It's a matter of allowing God, not emotion, to prompt the soul's decibels.

When the fragrance of the knowledge of God perfumes a moment in our lives, from our lips may flow rejoicings, or from our eyes quiet tears, solely for Heaven's notice. Laughter we can't silence, because we don't want to, may burst out of our souls. As we grow in Him, many great emotions will surface. They've been on hold within us, kept for the grand adventures of God discoveries. There we find just as He is God, He is radical, joyous fun! Psalm 16:11 says, 'in His presence is the fullness of of joy', a profoundly exuberant gladness! It can and it will still souls and chaos, and loose lips to a verbalized liberty!

Let the loud be the lauders. Let the calm of the quiet be a prelude to an unexpected and unsullied shout out, or a silence, in total reverence to God. And, let God be your God!

SOME THOUGHTS. . .

Isaiah 55:9 For as the heavens are higher than the earth, so are My ways higher than your ways, and My thoughts higher than your thoughts.
God thinks things out completely. He thinks things through. He considers every detail. Then, He calls us to trust His thorough thinking and well thought out plans. They will include a level of detail more extensive and comprehensive than anything we could ever conceive. He knows, has seen and has fully planned the absolute end from the very beginning.

By His omnipotence, He called into existence the stars, moon and sun, the universe, land and seas, and all things living and inanimate. He gave us life to live in the world. Yet, we doubt and question Him. Reluctantly, we trust Him, sorta.

To die to self is to divorce your flesh without any alimony payments. It's clearly a cut off, a complete detachment, with no misplaced compassion seducing you to regret.

When we see God correctly, we are able to come correct, be corrected, and appreciate correction.

Trying times are not times to quit trying, nor to try quitting!

I Declare. . . I will pursue God, I will yield to His will, and
I will trust His plan and purpose for my life.

Psalm 9:10 ~ Those who know Your name will trust in You,
for You, LORD, have never forsaken those who seek You.

Notes & Observations. . .

_____

_____

_____

_____

_____

_____

_____

_____

_____

_____

_____

_____

_____

DAY 9

GOD Is Loving, Kind, Merciful, And Just.

Let the morning bring me word of Your
unfailing love, for I have put my trust in
You. Show me the way I should go,
for to You I lift up my soul.
Psalm 143:8

PRAYER: Thank You, thank You, Lord,
for You! I am so grateful that You have
opened my heart and understanding to
You. My desire is to know You by heart,
and to please You with my life.

God, help me to love selflessly, beyond
me. Show me how to be compassionate,
sensitive, and merciful toward others, so
I can love as You do, without criticism or
judgment, hesitation or fear. Lord, thank
You for the privilege and grace of prayer,
to speak with You, knowing you hear me,
in Jesus Christ's name. . .

SOMETIMES. . . having faith is a workout, yet the greatest and most daring adventure of our entire life! Our pursuit after Jesus takes deliberate, mindful steps of faith and trust in Him.

Matthew 9:29b - According to your faith, let it be done. In Hebrews 11:6, we find it is impossible to please God without it. Our faith in God is the turnkey move to experience His power.

But faith is like a muscle. It has to be developed and strengthened, or it atrophies and grows weak. By reason of use, faith gets built up in a progressive, processive way. If we're willing to exercise faith, God will be pleased to grow our faith in Him.

When we have a need for something, or we want answers to problems, we engage faith. We *decide* to believe, expecting God to show up. This bravery baits an encounter with opposition, difficulty, or complication, AKA delay, where we must wait for an in-God's-time response. His Wait Room tests us and our growing, emerging faith, while unmasking a few anxious, questioning thoughts. But God tempers us with a cool down of surpassing-all-logic peace, a grace to help us see Him while we see no results. In the wait is where faith gains weight!

As our faith grows big, God delivers answers, #1. To match our purpose, best interest, or need, and #2. To exceed all we ask for! Trust in God's faithfulness, AKA His track record, is having strong, developed, efficacious, unwavering faith in God!

SOME PEOPLE. . . follow after Jesus because they are after something, but maybe not Him. They like all the fish sandwiches, and love His fabulous display of miracles, signs, and ta-da! They really want Jesus to do what He did, the supernatural stuff - shutting down stormy waves, raising up the dead, but not what He came to do: Change Them.

With eyes mesmerized, fixed on His show, many are missing the favor and blessing God is and has for them personally. As bad and missing is any real love for God. This prevents real regard for Him loving them, the only motive for all His acts. As well, they don't recognize His Lordship - Boss-ness, because their focus is only on His perfect performance of power.

What they need is that renewed, regenerated mind produced by the transforming power of God's Word. This changed mind speaks life to their lifeless thoughts and desires. It is a whole, holy mind that turns the empty of their souls into the true conviction of what is completely good and correct. A new mind is required to fully contain the revelation of God, His love, mind, and intentions for them, which are an unchanging constant!

Taking on this new mind looses the suddenlies of God's graces, causing them to know what they'd never known, regarded, or recognized before. It opens them to a new heart of love for God which becomes stoked to experience even more of Him.

The conviction of the soul, with its mind, will and emotion factors, leads to repentance, a true change of heart. Therein is a turning toward God with a focus on seeing Him for real, as He truly is: The loving God Who gave, and is giving still, to simply save us completely. Herein lies the motive for our requested, required obeisance to God, and our passionate desire for and pursuit after Him. It is the sole and absolutely pure reason for His call to us, His love for us, and our election to His family.

Philippians 2:5, 8b Let this mind be in you which was also in Christ Jesus... He *humbled* Himself and *became obedient* to the point of death, even the death of the cross. He did it for us!

The most profound performance and passionate display of the love of God ever accomplished was the Crucifixion. It is Jesus' ultimate sacrifice, and an unprecedented revealing of His heart. An incredible invitation comes with it: Receive My gifts - a new, changed life, a different appetite, a personal relationship, plus, the bonus of everlasting life in My House forever!

To get all the above, all the benefits, all the hugs and so sweet kisses of God, we gotta lay down our everything else which, by comparison, is zero, zilch, zip, nada, in a big'o, fat, empty bag. There is no better offer on the planet you can get without credit or a cover charge. It's fully paid for! Most amazing of all God's ta-da's is the recipient - the winner, takes all! O Hallelujah!

SOME THOUGHTS. . .

It's dangerous to allow your personal perspectives to hold
more weight than the truth.

Discipline is not the enemy of enthusiasm. It is the bouncer
of foolishness.

Unrighteousness gives the enemy legal access to your life.
Doing right with the wrong motive is, yep, unrighteousness.

As we grow in the knowledge of God, our depths of insight
and perception increase. This increase enables us to see
well what we were not able to see before, and know how to
use what we grew to see wisely and proficiently. Grow on!

Don't let your weekend faith experience disappear, without
a trace, all week long.

To be successful in your call, it's necessary to stay connected
to the Caller, your Source, or you may experience static with
reception, or an unfortunate interrupted or dropped call.

I DECLARE. . . I will keep my eyes on Jesus in order to see everything in the light of truth.

PSALM 46:1 ~ God is our refuge and strength, a very present and well proved help in trouble.

NOTES & OBSERVATIONS. . .

_____

_____

_____

_____

_____

_____

_____

_____

_____

_____

_____

_____

_____

DAY 10

GOD Is Never Angry With You, Nor
Is He Ever Disappointed In You.

I have come into the world as a Light, so
that no one who believes in Me
should stay in darkness.
John 12:46

PRAYER: O Lord, my God, please do in
me anything You need to do, so that You
can do through me everything You desire
to do. Draw me to You, Father. Fix me in
Your stability, Your plans, and Your ways.
You are the Potter, I am Your clay.

My God, please give me the grace I need
to follow You out of and away from things
unlike You. Shine Your Light on me, what
I do, my coming in, and going out. Father,
keep me close with my hand in Yours. My
thanks I give, in Jesus' name. . .

SOMETIMES. . . Christianity is a preference, like an item on a menu. But preference is not necessarily a conviction, a non-negotiable principle. Preference can change like an appetite. It can shift under pressure, or by persuasion, depending on one's desires, dietary restrictions, or what's on the menu, with all its descriptive, enticing selections.

But a preference could become a conviction to Christ depending on how He gets displayed, like items on that menu. If we sprinkle some savory salt of spiritual maturity, lots of personal submission, and a side of passionate pursuit of Jesus and His Word, that'll plate up quite nicely, and fully satisfy whosoever hungers and thirsts to taste and see God's goodness!

SOMETIMES. . . we come to the realization we *need* God! Therefore, to have more God, we need to *want* more God.

Actually, in this epiphany, God is saying we need to give Him more of us to avail ourselves to the privileges of His presence. It's an exchange, with the fabulous side effect of a better, and more rewarding relationship with God!

SOMETIMES. . . what is concealed behind locked, closed doors, trials, challenges, or extreme difficulty in acquiring full access, is great treasure waiting to be revealed.

SOME PEOPLE. . . get see sick. The problem is their lens is not cleared from the debris of their past mishandlings, inadequate training, brutal life experiences, and sad, bad things.

Because of faulty lenses, they can't tell what they're looking at is not what they think they see, nor is it all there is to see. See sickness is a blindness that develops when nurturing has had no entry, and reaching for new optics hasn't been explored, or been an option. Without vision, the desire to see perishes.

An interesting truth is hearing can help you see. But only when there's a willingness to know and receive truth to confront the issue, the see sickness. Point being, truth, when heard, can reveal the root cause of the malady, and bring to light the discolorations of the misinformings misconstrued as reality.

Light reveals truth that offers not only sight, but hearing to ears muted by the same debris. God respects our right to choose. However, if we decide on other than His directives, we'll gift a teaching opportunity to God Who so desires us to be spiritually current, correct, informed, healed, and clearly sighted.

We can do our thing, make our own choices, elect to stay as we are, blind and ineffective. But God will often hurt our eyes and our feelings since, in our temerity and ignorance, we hurt ourselves and delay our purpose. Remember Jonah?

See sickness is definitely a choice, but not a wise one. It's another stuck place of not-so-cozy comfort we decide to accept. Maybe we're okay with a handful of slightly-sightedness, but God has a whole field for us. Remember Ruth?

Remember Israel? They were spoiled in the wilderness with welfare takeout. Maybe they didn't get hungry enough for a little more, for the next level of living, for the next see level.

If we aim too low, God is not obligated to hand us grace. He's intensely interested in where we're destined to go, and getting us equipped to arrive there. Where we've been is of no import, but God is not okay with our see sickness. Sadly, if we're okay with it, we will forget to remember He IS The Healer.

Deciding to see will change our thinking, and our limiting, low vision. Sighted, we *will see* beyond what we saw. We'll be fit to become who God made us to be - seeing saints of God!

Agreeing with God is receiving sight to see as He sees, and to be as He is (1 John 4:17). That's a power to heal us, and clear away every trace of see sickness from our eyes, and our life.

1 Corinthians 2:9 Eye has not seen, nor ear heard, nor have entered into the heart of man the things which God has prepared for those who love Him.

SOME THOUGHTS. . .

Being a Christian is not a part-time, sometime, when-you-get-the-time job. It's a FULL time, every time, and all the time job, with the benefit of being able to call the Boss anytime.

If we stay too close to sin, and too familiar with sinners, we may engage in elements of compromise that can shade our integrity, scar our character, and assault our credibility. Oops!

Never bow to adversity.
Add some Verses to it, and see it bow to you.

Offense is like a spiritual hangnail. It's painful, irritating, ugly, and a trap of distraction. It snags the best relationships. It's a huge source of complaint, reactionary behaviors, prideful self-ishness, impatience, bitterness, insensitivity to truth, and hurt. It gives place for the enemy's constant harassment.

Getting over offense is a wise decision and a desirable feat. Staying out of offense is a power work of God's grace.

Hold on to the hope and promise that God's got something
for you, and it's not a hard time.

I DECLARE. . . Today I will make a difference in the world by being different from the world.

JAMES 1:12 ~ Happy is the one who endures testing, because when he has proven to be genuine, he will receive the crown of life that God promised to those who love Him.

NOTES & OBSERVATIONS. . .

_____

_____

_____

_____

_____

_____

_____

_____

_____

_____

_____

_____

_____

You are sent into the world to be

Salt - curing, seasoning it with taste, and

Light - turning off darkness, showing it the Way!

2ND

QUARTER

DAY 11

God Is The Answer To All We Will Ever Need.

O God, You are my God. Early will I seek
You. My soul thirsts for You, my flesh
longs for You in a dry and thirsty
land where there is no water.

Psalm 63:1

PRAYER: O Lord, You are everything to me,
my provision and answer, my peace and the
power I desperately need. You are my God,
my Father, and my All in all!

I thank You for never giving up on me, loving
me, keeping me every day and night. I want
to love You in return, each moment of all my
life, and give back every praise due You. My
desire is to honor You and please You, Lord.
With all my heart and strength, I give thanks
to You. In the strong name of Jesus Christ,
I pray, believe and expect. . .

SOMETIMES. . . things that affect us are simply congenital. Family challenges, illnesses, proclivities, environmental conditions, the 'what' that happened are a few of the issues waiting to inform us, and to be seen on us, on a regular basis.

These externals frame our movements, establish parameters, and make deposits in all our personal accounts without any endorsement, solicitation, or invite. They wait, lurking, looking to arrive on our turf in order to exhibit the power of their prowess and perpetuity, front and center, and way too close up.

The task, if we so choose to accept its mission, is to become the informer to these imposers, and the instructor of our own mind. Once we do, we grow to know what is on the inside of us - the Root, Jesus, the Christ, and His route for us, our life and our future. Armed with this birthright truth, we're enabled to open our mouths, filled with God's Word, and forth tell the instruction to thwart their generational and ill effects.

Though we're born into sin, destruction, maladies and trouble, no weapon formed will prosper (Isaiah 54:17) to prevent us or our mission. This grace protects our predestined and spoken by God life's purposes. His voice is sovereign over any, every, and all things that may come to oppose.

Our voice, aligned with God's Word, speaks with His same

timbre of authority. We speak to quell the congenital noisome residue left to distract us from our mission and freedom, to which we were born and called, and our exit from captivity.

Jesus, our Deliverer, desires our set freedom from every bondage and limitation. His works loosed us to receive His promise of real life. It is urgent, then, for us to commit to following His lead away from the enemy of our soul, and from our inner-me tendencies to reattach to any alluring flashbacks.

When we remain in Him and in pursuit of Him, and His Word remains in us, we become effulgently effective, while profoundly unaffected by the aggravations of opposition. We taste stability in the grace of having none of these things able to move us (Acts 20:24) out of our position, or our peace.

God made us to produce and increase in order for us to prosper and glorify Him in the process. That is a congenital condition of salvation's new birth. Our compliance and appreciation of His generosity are the passageway to the fullness of these, His benefits, and every one of His promises. Our response - our gesture of obedience, becomes an escape route to a newly founded identity, and a vision to see past the restrictions of what was. All together, and now, we have the rich, abounding, freeing, congenitally organic life Jesus came and gifted to us (John 10:10b), and that without measure!

SOME PEOPLE. . . have 'saved' tendencies. They are not fully committed to the whole idea, nor the full on responsibility of the Salvation Package, which includes full surrender.

SOME PEOPLE. . . want to see God manifested through your life, but, at the same time, they get upset with you when He gets evidenced, as in, He is 'seen' on you.
Maybe it's because all that Light kinda hurts their eyes.

SOME PEOPLE. . . ascribe to the idea of greatness, but shy away from its process: the intentionality, the disciplines, and the much diligence it takes to achieve it.
They get seduced by couches, TV's, and other lesser gods.

SOME PEOPLE. . . think 'train up a child in the way that he should go' (Proverbs 22:6a), means to lead them in the direction they, the trainers, have in mind.

SOME PEOPLE. . . view one season of your life as if they know you like a book. They misjudge, having not read nor taken into account all your chapters. But take no thought! Your Father God knows you, purposed you, and wrote your story.

SOME THOUGHTS. . .

Psalm 40:1-2 I waited patiently for the Lord and He turned to me, and heard my cry. He also brought me up out of a horrible pit, out of the miry clay, and set my feet on a rock, and established my steps.

God doesn't wait for us to get out of the pit, the incarceration, or the hot mess. He meets us in the confusion, in the problem, in the dilemma - to bring us up to standing.
He answers our call, and often before we call (Isaiah 65:24)!

It's not polite to complain about what we're praying about.

In our crisis, what we haven't thought of has been thoroughly, and completely thought through by God.

Favor, AKA grace, takes the 'earn' out of success, and the 'labor' out of increase.

Salvation is a gift that keeps on saving, rescuing, and freeing.

We were never, ever called to figure it all out. But, we are called to trust God (Proverbs 30:5)!

I DECLARE. . . Today I will make deposits of God's love as random, but deliberate, acts of kindness.

ACTS 1:8 ~ You will receive power when the Holy Spirit has come upon you, and you will be My witnesses in every place.

NOTES & OBSERVATIONS. . .

_____

_____

_____

_____

_____

_____

_____

_____

_____

_____

_____

_____

_____

_____

_____

DAY 12

GOD Loves You More Than Anyone Has Loved You, Can Love You, Or Ever Will Love You.

I sought the LORD, and He heard me, and
delivered me from all my fears.
Psalm 34:4

PRAYER: Holy God, how wonderful are You!
You consider me - You hear my prayers and
groanings, You have great concern for every
thing about me. Your patient, lovingkindness
is beyond my understanding. You love me so
well and so tender! Lord, You bring me to my
knees, even when I'm already on them.

God, I thank You for seeing me and knowing
every way within me. Your love has no limits
or conditions. Father, I so need You! Will You
teach me to love You better, and help me do
that well? I ask, in Jesus' name. . .

SOMETIMES. . . we create a blazing fire with our choices. What's so funny (NOT) is how surprised and shocked we get when we choke on the smoke. Why? We forgot to remember those little consequences that come with our absolutely unspiritual, unethical, ungodly, not to mention unwise and untimely, decisions. Perhaps 'de knee' time got deleted.

In our rush to be grown and on our own, we jes' assume we're free to do whatever we want to do. This attitude may abruptly shift into a less turgid one when we're faced with the realities of responsibility adulthood is s'posed to encompass.

An eye opening attitude adjustment is understanding that any independence we have, fa' real, lies in being completely and totally dependent on God. He's the only professional adult in any room we're in. Be His child! It's quite liberating. And, be wise: Let the Holy Ghost be your Smoke Detector!

SOMETIMES. . . we come out of where we came from and what we did, but where we came from and what we did have not yet come out of us. Oops!

Little by little, step by step, the faith walk leads us away from our dysfunctional familiars into the unknown and unfamiliar freedom God gifts to us. It's a liberty that allows us to be and to do what we never imagined we would be or do before.

SOME PEOPLE. . . are impatient and so easily frustrated. Their common excuse is they get irritated by the immaturity of other folk. But, if truth be told, it's really because *they* are immature, accompanied by a few sides of inconsideration, 'attitude', angst, and some not-so-very-nice ways of thinking.

At some point, everybody didn't know something, and had to grow to learn what it was they didn't know. It may have been humbling, or it might have been fun, to take that class and get smarter than the less learned. Choosing to learn is a maturity, a wisdom, and a strength that empowers us with reasonable sensibility toward others, and without eye cuts of criticism.

During the maturation process - our grow up season, wisdom arrives, infusing us with the counsel of understanding to help us apply what we learned to know. We glean, as we do so, a proper attitude and decorum devoid of derision, judgment, or arrogance toward anyone else's lack thereof.

Another amenity is a budding consideration that blooms once we arrive at this revelation: IF it had not been for God looking out for us, in the first dang place, there would've been no opportunity to grasp anything. Thank You, God, for a brain and its functionality! No one can boast because it's all God's grace and generosity *to us all*. No one can look down on anyone because God is mercifully looking down *on us all!*

Impatience cuts off those considered less, or weaker, like cutting off someone in traffic. Every person doesn't need to hang with every other person, but why disregard them? Maybe they have no personal significance to us, but God made us all significantly important to Him. His graciousness is the template.

When our eyes aren't tunnel visioned to *self*, a sense of oneness and sameness of equality bears the weakness of others without judgment. As we are one in His body, we rightly adjust to accommodate a weakness, or a difference, in order to help strengthen the whole body to wholeness. It takes wisdom, maturity, and God to see we *can* be a help by caring about others and their lives, or burdens, as God intentioned.

Just as we all have a measure of faith, God confers on every one a portion of gifts, ideally purposed to be interdependent on the gifts in others. It's how we get to function through our best capacities, *regarding each other* as a part of His body.

The grace of interdependence is a supernatural expression of God and His love for us. We need it to stay focused, effective, productive, connected, *patient*, and moving forward, making spiritual progress in all places, and together. His love empowers us to bear each other's burdens (Galatians 6:2). We are made to be His Body, knit together purposefully and perfectly. We're one with Him, a fitted, conjoined, unified, whole Body.

SOME THOUGHTS. . .

Sin is never inconsequential. Sin is not just an offense against God, it's an offense against you, your life, your family, your future, and whoever or whatever you're connected to. It's an action that deteriorates, destroys, and defiles you with decay, for the wages of sin is death (Romans 6:23). Scary!

Sin's destruction prevents right perspective, sound judgment, and wise choice. Not dealt with, justified sin distends its residue to further complicate your future and ability to live the life of grace Jesus came to gift. To justify sin is to use excuses, or place blame, for bad habits and behavior. It is agreement with the enemy and disagreement with God, causing a ripple effect, and contaminating every part of you and your life.

Sin can take a legitimate desire off course to use it in an illegitimate way. This is because sin employs a devious agenda, or malicious intent, like usury or fraudulent involvement, to take advantage of and deceive unsuspecting, trusting victims.

Sin can be big, or some small thing. A small hole in a boat can still cause it to sink. Do we sin, or live for God? Do we follow after Jesus Christ, or holla at the enemy as we wallow in our flesh? Deuteronomy 30:19b is keen, sweet counsel: I've set before you life and death, blessing and cursing... *choose life, that you and your children may live.* Amen!

I DECLARE. . . I am who God, my Father, says I am!

PHILIPPIANS 4:6 ~ Be anxious for nothing, but in everything
by prayer and supplication, with thanksgiving, let your
requests be made known to God.

NOTES & OBSERVATIONS. . .

_____

_____

_____

_____

_____

_____

_____

_____

_____

_____

_____

_____

_____

_____

_____

DAY 13

GOD Is Your How, Your Hope, Your Help, Your Healer, And You Are His Handiwork.

The earth is the LORD's, and the fullness of
it, the world and all they who dwell in it.
Psalm 24:1

PRAYER: Father, thank You for this day, for all You have given me - the great, the small, the challenge, and the victory. Thank You for making me Your child, giving me purpose to do great things in the earth that only You, O Lord, can bring to manifestation!

I appreciate You, and thank You for grace to accomplish what You've ordained, anointed, appointed, and predestined me to do. If You will, please help me to represent You well in excellence, and in honoring You with my life.
I pray in Jesus' great name. . .

SOMETIMES. . . we want God on 'our' side. But it's much more important that we're on His side. We certainly want God to bless what we're doing, yet that desire may be without realizing we need to be doing what God blesses.

How beautiful is God, Who loves to operate at our side, stand by our side, advocate for our side, and function through our lives to help us partner with Him, side by side.

SOMETIMES. . . we are like Paul as he was on his way to Damascus. His scene, his life, his journey changed, when, all of a sudden, he could not see (Acts 9:3-9).

God plans to encounter us, on our way down life's road, to demask us. It's a bit like it is in the theater when the lights go off, and you can't see anything. It's an indication that something is about to happen, the scene is about to change. We are, too!

If we know our lines, the Word of God, we'll find ourselves in a starring role, well lit, on point, in position, purpose aligned, at center stage, eyes wide open, clearly seeing very well.

SOMETIMES. . . God will give access to great favor from ungodly people, or those who don't like you. Sometimes, and cleverly, it will happen without them realizing it!

SOME PEOPLE. . . cause relationship rashes. Those unsightly blemishes are irritating to no end. They'll clear up fast when you cleanse and exfoliate, purging yourself of those irritants carried by the wonderful folk in said relationships.

As friendly, nice, and not all that toxic as they are, unfortunately, the astonishing, revelatory truth is that they don't mesh with your purpose. At best, they are simply seasonal.

Like Christmas ornaments adorning July, put them away by setting enforceable boundaries. While they may remain a part of your lifestyle - the carpool, gym or church you attend, you, your life and purpose are too valuable not to be guarded.

Of importance is halting the contaminates of their influences, habits, issues, and preferences. The portions they deposit in and on your life can subtly stain or divert God's personal path for you. Distractions, limitations, sidebars, or error, can be encumbrances you're not always able to see.

Think of the lobster in the cool water the heat slowly, and ever so gradually cooks. It's something you cannot allow nor afford to continue, even if it is on an extremely low simmer. NO!

Trust God, and thank Him for no more rashes! Keep a healthy, clean, fresh, cleared-up-for-purpose you everywhere you are.

SOME THOUGHTS. . .

When you are willing to do what you are called to do, but not qualified to do, your obedience *to the call* is your qualifier. It is God's grace that enables you to accomplish the task. Believe BIGGER! Water desires to be walked on again!

We will be filled with the Holy Spirit only as much as we are yielded to the Holy Spirit.

To be continually distracted is to be certainly defeated.

You are superior to your gifts, which is exactly why you should never, not ever, be driven by them.

Why are you backing down when God is backing you up?

The demographic of Scripture is not only of church ministers, leaders, apostles, clergy, pastors, evangelists, prophets, pew sitters, staff, teachers, and volunteers.

Scripture addresses the person of *every* believer, and speaks infallible truths to all unbelieving whosoevers.

I DECLARE. . . Today I will wear peace as a garment!

1 CORINTHIANS 6:20 ~ You were bought at a price,
so then, honor God in your body and in your
spirit, which are owned by God.

NOTES & OBSERVATIONS. . .

_____

_____

_____

_____

_____

_____

_____

_____

_____

_____

_____

_____

_____

_____

DAY 14

GOD Watches Over You With Love In His Eyes.

In peace I will both lie down and sleep,
for You, LORD, alone make me dwell
in safety and confident trust.
Psalm 4:8

PRAYER: God, I choose to trust You and follow Your lead. I love You because You first loved me. I believe You, for You have been faithful to bless me every day of my life. Lord, forever will I seek You!

Thank You for being with me and for me - in my good times, and not so good times, and in every season. No matter the issue, the what, the why, You are there with me. For all You do for me, for everything, I am grateful. Lord, I bless You today. I want to praise You to delight Your heart, now and always, in the name of Jesus. . .

SOMETIMES. . . we 'try to believe' God for what our faith and trust are yet a lil' too underdeveloped for.

It seems as if our tearful cries are flatly ignored, as though we didn't pray at all. Did He not hear all that conviction in our supplication? Why God doesn't answer faster, and with a big fat 'YES!', adds to our dismay, doubts, and doleful frustration.

Truth is revelatory! It seems His 'No' is because He loves us too much to allow us to hurt us. He knows if we're not able to sustain what we ask for, with our small, un-exercised faith, particularly when we hardly maintain what we do have. As we begin to recognize exactly where we are on our faith walk, we'll grow to know God's 'No' means something better and greater will show up later *if* our trust in Him shows up now.

Trust illumines God's divine wisdom and unconditional love. In the light, we see God always prepping us for more! It's a plan to keep us from the dangers of less than His best. He waits for us to see and know, to desire and expect His ultimate best. It's what a really good and loving Father always does!

To believe and trust God is to look up to Him, and to grow forth in Him, thereby enlarging our capacity of faith in Him!

Believe and trust Psalm 34:8, Oh, taste and see that the LORD
is good! Blessed is the one who trusts in Him.

SOME PEOPLE. . . have an inability to surrender to God. Whether strong-willed, wounded or wonky, their challenge to yield to any authority can be an extreme 'uh, no!'.

Some women, craving to be married to some knight in super shiny or very dull armor, are far, far away from any intention to submit to male authority. Is it rebellion or pride, a sign of weakness, or the result of bad experiences?

It's a deep seated issue when people are deftly loyal to their own desires and comfort. Someone else's desires will never reach their radar. The thought of submission to God's will is an uninterestingly foreign land to their minds.

This may stem from being oblivious to God's love, especially in a personal consciousness. If we never encounter His love, the ability to love selflessly may be an un-mined potential. A lack of willingness to submit, to God or anyone else, can develop internal struggles and relational conflicts.

James 4:7 texts: Submit to God, resist the enemy and he will flee. Folk submit to everything, resist God, and wonder why their blessings flee. Without submission, absolute yielding of the will and bowing of the heart, receipt of all that is needed to live life in full isn't sure. A rich lesson to submit and commit to learning is: The more you *yield*, the *more* you yield!

SOME THOUGHTS. . .

Your life should be a Declaration of Dependence on God.

Besides being a non-producer of any good results, worry adversely affects your heart, immune system, circulation, glands, nervous system, and it may cause hair loss.

Without mastery of the small things, there's no understanding and knowledge to manage the greater things.

Accountability is a real, true friend. It won't let you slide nor hide. It won't let you say or do any ol' thing, or act any way 'ya wanna' without bringing it to your attention, and calling you out on it. It's wholly committed to building your character, integrity, and worth. It's something you cannot succeed or lead without!

Self-control is the fruit of the Spirit.
Self-centeredness is the produce of the flesh.

God doesn't make us do anything. Yet, He does expect us to do something, and clearly something right well.

I DECLARE. . . I am victorious because God gives me the
wisdom and grace to always overcome.

PROVERBS 16:7 ~ When a man's ways please the LORD,
He makes even his enemies to be at peace with him.

NOTES & OBSERVATIONS. . .

DAY 15

*GOD Planned A Great Future For You Long
Before You Landed On The Planet.*

He put a new song in my mouth, a song of
praise to our God. Many will see and fear
the LORD and put their trust in Him.

Psalm 40:3

PRAYER: Thank You, God, for Who You are,
God alone! Thanks for being a Hearer and a
Doer of my words of prayer and supplication
to You. Thank You for the grace to become a
hearer and a doer of all Your Word.

God, I will sing a new song to You, with hope
of giving You due and acceptable praise and
honor. I will sing aloud, hoping that someone
will hear and come to know You, Your power,
Your love, and come to trust and believe You.
Please hear my heart, in Jesus' name. . .

SOMETIMES. . . God prunes us to bless us. He cuts things, and certain folk, off from access to us. He also moves stuff out of our reach that disregards or encumbers our purpose. God will prune off. By His grace, wisdom and love, we will grow on!

SOMETIMES. . . the Church, the Body of Christ, sequesters itself from the world, abandoning its purpose to be the salt and light, the solution and help, to the problems around it.

It's as if we are a gated community, protecting ourselves from those we're to commune with. Instead of being the answers to the people, we speak commentary on the problems, alienating God from them, and making His love for them irrelevant. It's as if Christ has left the building of our focus, getting dismissed by our lack of interest and intention, passion and pursuit.

The Church is *called* to see the world's need for God! It is our assignment to see the world transformed by Christ manifesting *through us*, His Body. God gets seen, and His power within us gets released to whosoever we touch. Did we forget to remember God never told the world to go to church? He did call the Church to go into all the world (Mark 16:15)!

Romans 8:19 confirms that the whole earth awaits, with eager longing, for the revealing of the sons of God. Open the gates! Ain't it time we showed up?

SOME PEOPLE. . . struggle with giving. They have a real problem with being generous. It's hard for them to share their time, talent, treasure, and, for a few, thank you's.

God's question in Malachi 3:8, 'can a man rob God?', should hopefully evoke a tidbit of conviction to those more tender to hearing Him. Pondering the question, however, might bring to mind the audacity of a robber, who definitely doesn't accident-ally rob since robbery is premeditated. And not just that scary part, it usually includes an intention to harm. Yikes!

Albeit, nobody can really harm God, or that person would be God. But if giving were reconfigured to the truth that whatever anyone has has been given them, directly or indirectly by God, then, perchance those purse strings would loosen to flow with some thanks added. Giving could be deemed an honor, and a more frequented response to receiving so much.

In reality, that purse and the hands holding it are gifts of facili-tation from the generosity of God. Gratitude has to appear es-pecially if the tag 'robber' is to be removed. Becoming more adept at giving can also result from being truly fluid at loving, only because you can't love without giving!

1 Corinthians 4:7b What do you have that you didn't receive? If you received it, why do you boast as if you didn't receive it? John 3:16 God so loved the world that He gave...

SOME THOUGHTS. . .

Disappointments come to 'dis' your appointment with great. They come, some by way of offense, others by way of mis- placed expectation, or folly. They come to distract and sub- tract from your efforts to advance, achieve, and accomplish.

By them, your effort and focus are abated from what you're called to. Because of them, you get redirected away from at- tending the appointment God scheduled. For sure, they are a captivity, a snare, and an attempted wounding of the heart.

But in your brave, decide to see the big picture which far sur- passes the small in the people, or the insignificance of the sit- uation imposing the injury. The good news is, God never con- demns the captive, but He will give the grace of freedom from harm. Just know, any disappointment is confirmation you've got greater worth than the time lost dwelling on the intended offense born of that *seeming* missed appointment!

Refresh, refocus, and fast forward: To new opportunities, To growth through it all, To grasping a better view of your value, and To appreciating God for blessing you beyond measure, which is the 'why' dis-er's show up to challenge.

Remember, God will never un-call you, which is the 'why' He restores and rebooks every appointment of purpose!

I DECLARE. . . I will follow after God Who leads me onto the paths of purpose, and out of the ways of darkness.

2 CORINTHIANS 3:17 ~ The Lord is the Spirit, and where the Spirit of the Lord is, there is freedom.

NOTES & OBSERVATIONS. . .

_____

_____

_____

_____

_____

_____

_____

_____

_____

_____

_____

_____

_____

_____

_____

DAY 16

GOD Is Salvation ~ Our Forever
Rescue And Help.

What, then, shall we say in response to
these things? If God is for us,
who can be against us?
Romans 8:31

PRAYER: Dear Almighty God! I must say
I'm so grateful You've given me a bravery
to believe and trust You! I know well, and I
confess, I can do nothing without You. It is
because of You, Lord, I can do all things in
Your strength and ability.

You've called me to good success so I may
honor Your name. You believe in me. I'm in
awe for You trust me to do what I know You
know I can't do without You. Lord, only You
can do the miraculous! I surrender my all to
You. My answer is, 'Yes, Lord', to Your call.
I pray in Jesus Christ's name. . .

SOMETIMES. . . we need to thank God BIG for answering the prayers we almost *didn't* have faith to pray! Those all over the top, long-shot prayers we were so scared to say out loud, fully doubting they'd be heard, let alone answered.

To think God would show up for us, especially for some of us not too holy ones, was unrealistic, a pipe dream, a far distant landing. Nonetheless, out of His great love for us and a desire to be there, not just as omnipotent but as an amazing Parent, He did, He does, and He will again, and again.

If God answered Joshua's request to make the sun stand still (Joshua 10:12-14), and King Hezekiah's supplication to have a sundial move backwards (Isaiah 38:7-9), what's a little trust in our long-shot, lookin' so impossible asks for God's intervention? He's the same yesterday, today and forever, and no respecter of any person! Why not expect Him to answer, just like they did? And thank God He included a few crises moments in the Bible to help us believe, know and trust He's not only able, but He's a willing, always good Father. As *He said* to Abraham in Genesis 18:14, "Is there anything is too hard for the LORD?"

Mark 9:23 All things are possible for the one who believes! So like Joshua, meet God with courageous, bold faith, and expect Him to show up with a supernatural response. It's simple: Ask, Seek, Knock, Believe, Trust, and W-A-I-T for it!

SOME PEOPLE. . . want to move from faith to power, but *before* they're fully processed for power. What's a must is developing enough Christ-measured, faith-initiated character to temper personal behavior and accountability, while having a solid acumen for managing weighty responsibilities.

To move prior to process only produces confusion, painting underdeveloped pictures of God in them, and on their premature attempts to accomplish not-yet-God-endorsed works. BE still.

SOME PEOPLE. . . try to impress others with what they do, forgetting they can inspire and encourage many by sharing the wondrously marvelous and impressive things God has done.

SOME PEOPLE. . . subject themselves continuously, and religiously, to taking the wrong calls. As a result, they get sidebarred into various situations that drain their energy and disrupt their peace. Before they realize it, they are on the hook, again! They are on to give or do what they had never planned. So not wise since they were well aware of the folk who called, with their always-not-fun, persistent problems.

Somehow they forgot about Caller ID, a gift that's a wisdom and a grace we can never live home without!

SOME THOUGHTS. . .

Psalm 119:130 The entrance of Your words gives light, it gives understanding to the simple. How beautiful is that! We get to see plainly and clearly because the light is on.

Look at the generosity of God! He not only shares His heart in His words, but He adds illumination to them for whosoever will want to understand them and Him more deeply. We get to experience the depth within His words given to bring to flame our spirit. We get to behold what far exceeds the normalcy of the natural to see the invisible, the supernatural. We get provoked and stoked to be motivated to believe and do the impossible!

God, because He's just so dang cool, speaks His Word, planting Himself inside our soul. We need to and must grow closer, as in relationship, for His word-seed to impregnate its power within and germinate to fully develop, nurture and nourish us.

How blessed are we to receive His words, for they are Himself. Embracing the Word of God is like hugging God because it's not ink on a page, but it is God Almighty in print!

God seeks a person who will become a people. He calls within them future generations who will confer His Spirit of Grace to further produce His purposes, and thus build His Kingdom.

I DECLARE. . . I'm free to be who I am while I'm growing to become who God created me to be.

PSALM 66:1-2 ~ Make a joyful shout to God, all the earth! Sing forth the honor of His name, make His praise glorious.

NOTES & OBSERVATIONS. . .

_____

_____

_____

_____

_____

_____

_____

_____

_____

_____

_____

_____

_____

_____

_____

DAY 17

GOD Cannot Lie Or Deceive, Nor Bait And Switch.

By steadfast love and faithfulness, iniquity is
atoned for, and by the fear of the LORD
one turns away from evil.

Proverbs 16:6

PRAYER: God, Your mercies are new daily!
So everyday I will praise You with my whole
heart. Your constant impartations of wisdom,
understanding, and knowledge are profusely
and continually poured out to me, my Lord!

I offer my thanks to You from the sun's rising
to its setting. You are worthy of all my praise.
Your favor and providence have no measure.
Your graces of generosity are wonders to my
life. O Father, I am amazed by Your love and
every kindness. Forever I will be fully mindful
to be so very grateful! All my heart and focus
are Yours, in Jesus' name. . .

SOMETIMES. . . the Word of God challenges our issues. The Word confronts, and it can make us uncomfortable. Like a skin graft for a burn recovery, it's irritating, it itches, and it can hurt. It may sting a bit, but oh, it heals!

The Word declares of itself in Hebrews 4:12, For the Word of God is living and active, sharper than any two-edged sword, piercing to the division of soul and spirit, of joints and of marrow, and discerning the thoughts and intentions of the heart.

The Word cuts, severing antitheticals to our faith. It reveals, convicting our mind with inerrant, transforming truth!

SOMETIMES. . . experience can be stifling, and so un-fresh. It can be overrated, keeping what we do know preeminently in our mind. It can obstruct, preventing our learning what is new, current, relevant, different, and forward.

SOMETIMES. . . the power of faith is not in your prayer or your praise alone. The power is in *faith walking around*: Your wall, mountain, or impossibility, The obstacles in front of you, What you don't see, know or understand, Every negating 'No' from the voice in your head and the doubts in your soul. The power is in *your walk of faith*, mouth closed, in obedience and in trust, with a grateful heart of expectation.

SOME PEOPLE. . . have a tendency to outright misread, or personally interpret what God says in the Bible. What *they* see or don't see factors in. How they were raised or trained up may also sway. Issues, tastes, and other variegated elements justify their pit bull grip on an 'owned' understanding.

Human nature has a proclivity to infiltrate individual familiarities into a situation without just consideration of the actual parameters of the reality. A rush to conclusion, an assumption, an understanding, or lack there of, dilutes the Word's content, and perverts the context of God's intention.

To believe in God is awesome, but that's just the beginning of a bold, effective faith in Him. The faith walk is never a skip-to-ma-loo fancy dance. It is actual submission to God's Lordship, unwavering trust in Him, and true followship after Him. These steps conjoin, meshing into a determined commitment to believe and to know God, His Word, and His will.

In our highest degree of smart, we, the created, will never be more brilliant than our Creator. God, by His Spirit, will reveal what He has spoken to us by the Word. If we submit to listen, we will hear and know the truth, which includes a set-you-free bonus: *Release* from the error and bondage of our own understanding and misunderstanding, mistaken concepts, and, of course, those preconceived, wrong notions!

What we do or don't understand in Scripture is never for any private interpretation. Without the truth and revelation from the Holy Spirit, we cannot fully grasp the Word. The information is spiritual even when it applies to our natural lives. For it is *only* by the Spirit we are able to live a spiritual life by faith in God, and never by natural sight, other senses, or our mind.

Studying the Word proves and reproofs us, and our motives. Hebrews 4:13 is so clear, telling us nothing and no one is hidden from His sight. All things and all peoples are open and naked to His eyes. In truth, the Word proves itself and God's intentions, because the Word of God *is* God (John 1:1).

Walking in faith, pursuing God, and hearing His Word speak truth, are a multifaceted, soul stirring reality. Its all encompassing effect is as visual, emotional, mental, and physical, as it is spiritual. We get to experience God within our whole being, following His lead, on our journey to *His life*. It is He, the Master Mind, Who gifts us His Word. He lovingly shares its revelation and truth so we don't have to figure things out for ourselves.

1 Corinthians 2:14 But the natural man does not receive the things of the Spirit of God, for they are foolishness to him, nor can he know them, because they are *spiritually discerned*.

Matthew 22:29 Jesus replied, "You are in error because you do not know the Scriptures or the power of God."

SOME THOUGHTS. . .

To access the land, the promise, the promotion, the gifts, the big, *without* the conviction of accountability to occupy that place, will mean a move *out*, not forward.

Christianity should always be demonstrated, never dictated. In other words, did anybody actually see Jesus when they saw you, or did they only hear about Him?

Though the story of what you went through is beyond belief, share it as a testimony and a celebration of your survival!

Dreams and visions are prophetic pictures of your next level that don't match anything you know. A new, next level mindset is needed, for you must imagine 'there' before you get there.

Blame empowers those you blame with power over you. When you take ownership, you take back power.

Your pit is your personal training.
Your prison is your preparation for the wisdom of experience through which you will bring freedom to others.

I DECLARE. . . I walk by faith! I will not be moved by any ocular evidence, facts or circumstances that contradict.

PSALM 119:37 ~ Turn my eyes from looking at worthless things, and give me life in Your ways.

NOTES & OBSERVATIONS. . .

_____

_____

_____

_____

_____

_____

_____

_____

_____

_____

_____

_____

_____

_____

_____

DAY 18

GOD Answers Before We Call Because He Longs To Be Gracious To Us.

For the LORD gives wisdom. From His mouth
come knowledge and understanding.
He guards the paths of justice, and
preserves the way of His saints.

Proverbs 2:6, 8

PRAYER: My Lord and my God, You're the
only living God. You are Almighty, and more
than good. My praise and thanks are Yours!
You bless me in every moment of my day, in
every minute of my night. You're my Source,
my Peace, my Help, and my Hope.

Lord, You are the strength I need, and Who I
long for. Thank You for the grace, the mind to
know my life, homage, and gratitude are only
for You! I bless You and I praise You, O God,
in Jesus' wonderful name. . .

SOMETIMES. . . scars are scary! It's because they carry memories of pain, frightful experiences, or possibly, some embarrassing shame. Needful to say, we don't have to be afraid, nor do we need to be ashamed of our scars.

Before they were scars, they were wounds. But now, they are healed. They're here to remind us, regardless of what caused the marring that still remains, we remain alive to live.

Let the scars speak our victory. Let them recount our strength and faith, our courageous and new capacities, wrought out of the fray, that we never had before. Please, let them profusely speak out loud of the peace we now hold, stilling the noise of what was, and what may not have been right or good.

Jesus was at peace with all His triumphant scars. He allowed Himself to be touched in the place of His former pain, giving us a bravery amidst our own difficulties and vulnerabilities.

He is well acquainted, and shares with us our every scar, pain, and tear. He only asks we share His victory!

Isaiah 53:4a, 5 He (Jesus) has borne our griefs and carried our sorrows... He was wounded for our transgressions, crushed for our iniquities, upon Him was the chastisement that brought us peace, and with His wounds we are healed.

SOME PEOPLE. . . don't know God loves them fa' real! Most have heard, 'For God so loved the world...' (John 3:16). But they didn't get the memo about His uniquely personal, extremely lavish, specific and individual love *for them*.

Lots of folk think God is mad at them. To others, He's much too busy running the universe, being CEO of all creation, to take note of them in any big, fat, loving, considerate way.

The problem for both: They don't know God, and nobody told them. They've felt insignificant, missing out on being identified and accepted as a child of God. That's so hurting. It is the farthest thing from truth, and His heart of love for them.

God's priority is relationship. He desires we know and experience Him as a Father, and know who we are *to* Him - His children! God knows us (since He made us), and always reaches out to connect with us. He's aware of our abasing identity crisis and our lack in knowledge, for both affect our entire life.

God's Word to us is The Truth we must take to heart, just as a baby takes of his mother's breast to suckle.

Romans 8:21 Creation will be liberated from its bondage and brought into the freedom and glory of the children of God.

1 John 3:1 See what kind of love the Father has given to us, that we should be called *children of God*.

SOME THOUGHTS. . .

Never let your sight cloud your vision.

Sight can distract you with what you see, or fail to see.
      Sight is in the eye, but vision is in the heart.

Sight can shroud vision, while vision may contradict what
      you actually see in your eye's sight.

Vision precedes opportunity, and buoys your efforts toward
      its accomplishment.

Check your eyes often. But more frequently, examine your
      vision to discover what's in your heart.

Adversity enlarges your faith while closing the gap between
where you are and where God is growing you to be.
Its testing qualifies you for your next level.

Pressure can magnify the problem.
Worship will always magnify the Answer.

The faith walk may be the slowest mode of transportation,
      but it's the most certain way to arrive.

Being understood is so much better than only being heard.

I DECLARE. . . I will value and esteem myself that I may impart value and esteem to others.

PROVERBS 29:25 ~ The fear of man brings a snare, but whoever trusts in the LORD shall be safe.

NOTES & OBSERVATIONS. . .

DAY 19

GOD Is Always With Us, Even When We
Are Far Away From Him.

You have kept record of my wanderings.
You put my tears in Your bottle, counting
each of them. When I pray, LORD, then my
enemies will retreat, for I know for certain
You are with me. I trust You, and I am not
afraid. No one can harm me.

Psalm 56: 8-9, 11

PRAYER: Lord, You are glorious! You are
wonderful! Your considerations of me and
my concerns, my hopes and relationships,
my dreams, my life, and my future are too
great, and much more than I can fathom.

I praise You for never leaving me without
Your peace, hope and confidence. Where
can I go that You're not there? My Father,
I appreciate Your always-ness to me. It is
in Jesus' great name I pray. . .

SOMETIMES. . . you have to ignore what you're hearing. Mark 5:35-36 makes it plain: While He was still speaking, some came from the ruler's house who said, "Your daughter is dead. Why trouble the Teacher any further?" As soon as Jesus heard the word that was spoken, He said to the ruler of the synagogue, "Do not be afraid, *only believe.*"

When you really know God, you will hear and know His still, small voice over the noisy, distracting chaos of fraudulent half-truths, facts, insults, opinions, and intimidating innuendo.

Whose report will you believe? Have faith in God, Who never lies, and Who always has Good News of help and hope!

SOMETIMES. . . it's better to leave a position open, or the task undone, than to designate the wrong person for the seat of assignment, power or purpose. It's Wait Room time!

Before the one considered takes the chair, there needs to be a 'want to' within them. If not, there's waste in effort, with added loss of time, energy and fiscal investment. It is impossible to make anyone responsible for anything they have no desire to do, or initiative to make happen, nor capacity to accomplish.

Take heart! It is a tutorial in trusting God to do His will of purpose while you glean wisdom and gain faith in the wait.

SOME PEOPLE. . . are way too busy to obey God. Busy, as in, washing their cars and nets, doing their careers and lives, focusing on what they think they know and like. They BE busy! To them, God's requests and commands are impositions, or maybe, just too complicated to 'ad-hear' to.

Other folk are too smart or too proud to obey. To them, the ways of God are rigid, kinda unreasonable, not to mention inappropriate to their lifestyle. To them, His ways don't always make sense. These sweet lil' critters neglect to consider, as smart as they are, God's ways are higher and smarter!

What too many don't realize is that twice, in Proverbs 14:12, and 16:25, the Text Message says, 'there is a way that *seems* right to a man, but its end is the way of death' (YIKES!). While too busy, proud or smart, it is of great import to know neglect is a disobedience, which makes it outright sin (Uh oh!).

No matter what, God always knows what's best (He IS God, and highly intelligent!). Obeying Him may not be 'the' latest social media thing to do, but it's certainly the most wise and prudent, especially if Heaven is to be your forever home!

Bottom line: #1. Just obey, even when you don't believe, trust, or know the outcome. The dealio is, your faith may be weak, but your obedience will always bless you. Think on Abraham.

He obeyed when God's request for his son, Isaac, was way far from reason (Genesis 22). That's some fa' real trust!

#2. Let God's Word supersede your logic, excuses, feelings, plans, and agenda. The Word (Bible) is over 2,000 years old, it's still alive, and it works. How old are you?

#3. God promises to bless people when they obey. In Luke 5 is the story of the disciples' failed attempt at fishing all night, and Jesus telling them to try it again. When they obeyed His instruction, they caught a massive amount of fish. What are you trying to catch, or attempting to do?

God is aware of you, your heart, your good-bad days, issues, fears, likes and dislikes. Yet His love for you doesn't stop nor change *while* He's waiting for you to wake up to change.

Just hear Him out! You'll become more aware of Him. Then His heart will overwhelm you and gift you with a sensitivity to Him that will bring you to your senses, and your knees. Yep, it may seem scary, but it's a lot cooler than hell!

One of the greatest benefits of obedience is that it causes you to *know* God better. In that place you'll find Him lovingly giving you every grace *needed* to obey. Within obedience is power. It's the message of freedom to become more than you would on your own, and to arrive way ahead of your present you!

SOME THOUGHTS. . .

Jewelers deliberately cut facets into precious stones to cause
light to better display their spectacular beauty.
Adversities, betrayals, and challenges create facets within us,
allowing our light to shine a brilliant beautiful!

We weren't taught enough that God is approachable, not mad
at us, loves us individually and uniquely, and by His pursuit,
expresses His desire for relationship with us. Who knew?

What didn't happen can be as catastrophic as what did!

A good relationship is a gift of love, trust and commitment that
gives, prospers, grows and progresses.
If any of that is missing, rethink the relationship, and perhaps,
consider counseling, or an exit strategy.

The greatest breakthrough is when truth breaks through your
mind, and you begin to think correctly.

Faith is believing, obeying, trusting, and patiently waiting.
It is never analyzing, questioning, doubting, stressing, crying,
worrying, complaining, and whining.

I Declare. . . The everlasting, ever loving, eternal God,
Who has no rival, is my Father.

Proverbs 1:7 ~ The fear of the LORD is the beginning of
knowledge, but fools despise wisdom and instruction.

Notes & Observations. . .

_____

_____

_____

_____

_____

_____

_____

_____

_____

_____

_____

_____

_____

_____

_____

_____

_____

DAY 20

God Gives Abundant Wisdom To Whosoever Will Ask For It.

But the one who looks into the perfect law,
the law of liberty, and perseveres, being
no hearer who forgets, but a doer who
acts, he will be blessed in his doing.
James 1:25

PRAYER: My Lord, Your Word is the light
I need on this path of faith to live life right.
God, thank You for Your standard of order
helping to govern my choices. It is by You
I am enabled in all manner of wisdom.

Father, as well, I need Your grace to keep
me faithful and focused. I desire Your help
daily to stay mindful of You and honorable
to Your principles and purpose in my life. I
ask You in faith, my God, and in the name
of Christ Jesus, the Lord. . .

SOMETIMES. . . our theology slips into ritual mode. It can easily become a tradition, the thing we do to 'feel' like we are spiritual, mostly because it was so much a part of our history. Thus, we attend our religious establishments from habit, as a duty, or as CEO's (Christmas, Easter, and okay-I'll-go visitors), instead of people seeking an encounter with God.

The oppressive problem with personal theology, AKA one's belief system, B.S., for short, is its potential to desensitize us to a genuine spirituality, quelling our desire for a vibrant connect to God. Because of varied philosophies, religious ideologies, and other B.S.'s, which are usually subtly devoid of the Word's full truth and power, many are unaware real relationship with God is doable, let alone His desire. Sadly, few haven't so much as heard God loves them not only unconditionally, but personally, and as uniquely individually as they are. Is that not crazy good, and awesomely amazing?

In today's culture, spirituality has been reduced to the mentality of 'to each his own', and 'this is how we do it', which may or may not include God. Independence, intellectualism, and individuality line the paths of thought more than ever. Entering the supernatural in the arena escalates the moment to an event, an episode of entertaining enlightenment, rather than the elevation of our spirit and soul for our life's edification. To shift all this, we need to *receive* a real manifestation of God's power!

This means becoming open, beyond our reasoning, to what's not natural. We will need to be open to new narratives, fresh knowledge, and legitimate revelation informing us of what we do not know. God's desire is for us *to desire* this openness to see His power displays not as great shows He produces, but as God *present,* to transform us from the inside out.

The point, for full effect, is to take a necessary risk. This may mean getting past and abandoning our B.S., our theological, so-not-fresh tradition, and opening up to a spirituality that has nothing to do with religion, but all to do, and rapt, with God.

Next is a disconnect from reason and religion, and a real hook up to the why we are on the planet: #1. To know God, His love, and His purpose for our life, #2. To believe He will enable us to become who we were born to be, and #3. To experience the reality of both requisites for God and His glory, for the fulfilling of our abundant life destiny, and for the sake of others!

Faith in God is belief anchored in God, and in all He is. We become His own relationally and discover He made us to be as He is in the earth, completely by His grace and our faith!

There's a measure of faith laying dormant within us that, when awakened, will lean us toward God like a plant leans toward the light. We will become boldly believable, without reason, religion or ritual, and fructuously, contagiously LIT!

SOME PEOPLE. . . bail from all the rules of Christianity. While they still wear the Club Tag, Christian, they have a problem with committing to the required reading of Holy Writ. The many do's and don't's find them omitting, even evading, the Text Messages, and missing the love in God's Love Letter!

Not being well read, they're not aware: The Law wasn't given 'to keep', for God knows well our inabilities in this area. What's clever and kind of God, He gave the Law to point out *to us,* #1. What's 'in' us, and #2. The truth of our need for Him to get that out of us. No laws, rules or regulations produce freedom or deliverance, change or empowerment. God alone brings all that, for He's great at it, and He longs to be the Help we need.

The grace of righteousness, to do what we don't have the will or ability to do, can only be received by faith, and by acting on that faith. It's by faith we must believe *and* receive what Jesus did, does, and will do *to undo* what we did, and are kinda, or mostly, still doing. At the intersection of God's grace and our faith, we morph into His righteousness that stands us upright *in* Him. We transform, we change, right before our eyes.

Righteousness is *God in us*, working through us, changing us into the image, likeness and mindset of Christ's Person. It's all God and His grace. It is never our perfect performance of the do's and don't's. What a liberty! What a love! What a God!

SOME THOUGHTS. . .

God makes a way out of no way because: #1. He loves you, #2. He can, and #3. His way is en route to your purpose.

Dwell on what's on the inside - your God, His Word, and truth, not what's on the outside - your stuff, opposition, and opinion.

Each battle and challenge, every difficulty and trial bring new strengths, power, wisdom, greater capacities, and deeper
levels of spiritual prowess and revelation.
Within them all are lessons to be gleaned to build greater faith
in the one who treads those fields of learning.

Thanks giving is a perennial attitude that blooms wildly colorful flowers of appreciation, drenched in the decadent fragrance of gratitude, and is host to lovely overtones of humility.

Never minimize yourself to fit other folk's view of you.
It is a dishonor to have a low vision of yourself, distorting your view of you, to accommodate someone else's discontent, insecurity or issues. See, be, and show up as The Best You!

Give God your reins to be loosed from the enemy's leash.

I DECLARE. . . God protects me and provides for me. God directs my steps and maintains my life.

GALATIANS 5:1 ~ For freedom Christ has set us free! Stand firm therefore, and do not submit again to a yoke of slavery.

NOTES & OBSERVATIONS. . .

SELAH. . .

Pause, and calmly think on these things!

HALF TIME

Have Time With God Who Has Given

You All The Time You Have!

3RD

QUARTER

DAY 21

GOD Is Our Source Who Supplies
All Our Resources.

Him (Jesus) we proclaim, warning everyone
and teaching everyone with all wisdom, that
we may present everyone mature in Christ.

Colossians 1:28

PRAYER: God, hallowed be Your Names!
You are my Father, Friend, Healer, Peace,
Provider, Comforter, Protector, Savior, my
Answer, and my Source of all supply! You
graciously and generously fill me with all I
have and more than I need.

Thank You for the knowledge of You in my
life, and its utterance on my lips. Great are
You, Lord, Your love, Your kindnesses and
grace. I'm scarcely able to speak, my King,
yet, I offer these words of thanks to You, in
Jesus' wonderful name. . .

SOMETIMES. . . you need new eyes to see. It's the onliest way you'll be able to see past all the puzzle pieces of your life to get the whole, panoramic view of you. It is the best way to understand all the good and all the bad blend together, weaving a tapestry of profoundly purposed, multifaceted beauty.

New eyes help you look at a rejection as not only protection, but a direction away from a disregard. Whether the disregarder is intentional or not, you get to walk past the not-so-nicety unstained, by the fabulous grace of God!

Even a full, lit moon is only seen in part. With both eyes open, then, examine to consider the whole picture of you, including the dark, unlit, questionable, suspect parts not fully disclosed or developed. You might find, upon closer inspection, real answers and explanations which clear your mind, and quiet your own insecurities about you. The discovery of whatever may or may not be aimed against you is your chance to see the love and graces of God show up on you, landing in splendid array! The colors, patterns and designs, created just for you, are the gifts and artwork He crafted on the canvas of your life.

Seeing the total picture is the door to truth, freedom and understanding. New eyes see new. You'll see you better than ever, because you *are* better than ever. This means you'll draw new haters, like moths to a flame, to confirm your light's brilliance!

SOME PEOPLE. . . are addicted to hearing and hearing the Word of God, but not as attracted to doing and doing the Word.

SOME PEOPLE. . . do social media and their phone alone. But when trouble comes, they call on God fast for some help! Because He's kind, with a magnitude of merciful generosity to extend to *whosoever dares believe*, He will answer that call!

SOME PEOPLE. . . think they're much smarter than those they prey on to take advantage of. They'd be smarter to simply utilize, #1. The purposed opportunity the preyed on present *for* their advantage, and #2. These overlooked wisdoms: A. God is not mocked. You will reap whatever you sow (Galatians 6:7)! B. The least you do, or the most you do to others is counted as *done to God* (Matthew 25:40, 45). Stay Woke!

SOME PEOPLE. . . suffer from an imposed identity crisis. They allow other people to tell them who they are, or are not. What slipped their minds, in the fray of their displacement, is they are children of God, and He has seated them in heavenly places, next to Him (Ephesians 2:6). They need to hear His still, small voice over the noise of accusation and put downs saying, with great affection, 'You are My beloved child!'

SOME THOUGHTS. . .

Psalm 147:3 God heals the brokenhearted and binds up their
        their wounds, curing their pains and sorrows.
God takes note of our broken places and knows every frac-
tured part. He's fully aware of our witherings, losses, griefs
and hurts. Because His love for us is complete and unfailing,
He will cure us to mend us in every place we allow Him in.

When we bare our heart, fears, secrets, and never before revealed devastations, God will by no means hurt, shame or rid-
icule us. Matthew 12:20 texts: A *bruised reed* He won't break,
a smoldering wick He will not quench, till He brings justice and
victory. People of purpose are certain to experience challenge,
but triumph is theirs for trusting God in and through difficulty.

God, the Healer, Fixer, and Restorer, rewards those who diligently seek after Him (Hebrews 11:6). We must believe and
know He has and is everything we need to be well, and to do
well our purpose. Both 'well' elements are a greatness that
draws opposition to wound, *and* God's power to heal! YAY!

Seeking God, the Giver of all purpose, to accomplish purpose,
positions us to be the rewarded recipients of His every grace!
By these graces we can be and do all things pertaining to our
purpose, and all those things extremely well. That's very cool!

I DECLARE. . . I have decided to be better than I was so I
can become the best I will ever and always be.

ISAIAH 26:3 ~ You will keep him in perfect peace, whose
mind is stayed on You, because he trusts in You.

NOTES & OBSERVATIONS. . .

DAY 22

*GOD Is He From Whom Comes All Wisdom,
Knowledge, Intellect, And Ability.*

I am the Alpha and the Omega, the Beginning
and the End, says the Lord God, He Who
is and Who was and Who is to come,
the Almighty, Ruler of all.
Revelation 1:8

PRAYER: Father, no one compares to You!
You made the moon, the stars, and the little
baby. Thank You, for now You're making me
all that I can be! Because of You, I am well,
and I am well able.

I choose alignment with You and Your Word.
I will seek You first for all my decisions. I will
pursue You deliberately to be the Counsel in
my life and my endeavors! I want You as the
Center of my life. I'm thankful for every thing,
and for every grace, in Jesus' name. . .

SOMETIMES. . . we wait on God in fear. But God will wait till things get bad somethin' fierce before He shows up.

That's because He's BAD, The Baddest! Our God is Terrible! Who or what can question or call Him on the carpet? So, uh, WHY fear folk, stuff, the enemy, opposition, or any challenge?

Psalm 47:2 For the LORD most high is terrible; He is a great King over all the earth (which He also owns!).

Psalm 66:5 Come and see the works of God: He is terrible in His doing toward the children of men (HA!).

Isaiah 41:10 Fear not, there's nothing to fear, for I am with you... for I am your God. I will strengthen you and harden you to difficulties, yes, I will help you, yes, I will hold you up and retain you with My victorious right hand of justice (OKAY?!).

FYI, God says 'fear not' over and over again, about 365 times in the Bible. WHEN will we actually believe Him?

SOMETIMES. . . a dark place can be the birth canal to your next level of increase, power, and victory.

Very often, growth takes place in the dark, much like planting a seed in soil. For optimum growth potential, be certain to note that dark place. Though unfamiliar, it should always be on your path to purpose, not a self-directed detour to some lil' garden that looks curiously lovely, but kinda shady!

SOME PEOPLE. . . *choose* to be victims of life. They get comfy with being victimized by their circumstances, and good at victimizing others by their state of mind. They make it not so comfy, fuzzy and safe to love them, or live with them.

Because of their martyr mentality, they're in constant receive mode, to get and be given to, for their own advantage rather than for the sake of community, and hardly for reciprocity.

As a result of thinking they're entitled to all they get, their laser like focus is set on getting something from anyone, everyone, or whosoever will hand it over. It's because they are, after all they've been through, poor and hurting victims of life.

Sadly, these victims refuse the victory given them by the One Who *was* martyred for us all. Prayerfully, they will grow to receive the unwritten verse which sayeth: "Gettest thou overeth it, in the name above all your circumstances, Jesus!"

SOME PEOPLE. . . are burdened with life's responsibilities and cares, but are negligent with the responsibility and care of relationship with God. The truth that's manageable weight is a connection to God. It is the most vital and important focus in all of life, especially since He's The Way, The Truth, The Life, and ALL The Help that's ever needed in life! Selah!

SOME THOUGHTS. . .

God places certain people in our lives to be trainers, teachers, encouragers, scaffolding, guideposts, and way markers. Their appointment with us is to point us toward God and purpose.

Often we mistake their information and wisdom as being 'their' opinion, judgment, criticism or naivety. By this summation, we decide to refuse to hear or appreciate them for being the gift they are. Whether awkward or eccentric, their outward appearance may draw an infusion of our personal, opined critiques. So to protect our ego from their goading, we keep us safe, far away from seeing the depth of their worth and task.

Falling into this trap, this snare of the fowler, is meant to clog our ears, blind our eyes, and ultimately stymy our growth. It means we operate in deficit, the less than plan. But when we return to wisdom, and our senses, God is gracious to forgive, to regift, and to recalibrate our tutorials of direction.

Decide to take advantage of an extended handrail. It's a priceless gift within their wraps, no matter how fraught the encounter, or how painful to pride it is to 'take' their truths. We should intend to never take for granted the grace-lets God expresses through those He purposefully sends our way. His graces may show up as unexpected, foreign, cool, huge, raw, unique, or amazing! All are to be graciously and gratefully received!

I DECLARE. . . Today I confess that I know God is for me.

PSALM 36:7 ~ How precious is Your lovingkindness, O God!
Therefore the children of men put their trust under
the shadow of Your wings.

NOTES & OBSERVATIONS. . .

_____

_____

_____

_____

_____

_____

_____

_____

_____

_____

_____

_____

_____

_____

_____

DAY 23

GOD Is In Our Emergencies, In Our Urgencies,
And In All Our Life's Entries.

The LORD, He is the One who goes before you.
He will be with you, He will not leave you nor
forsake you. Do not fear nor be dismayed.

Deuteronomy 31:8

PRAYER: Lord, You are my God Who is able
to make all grace abound to me in every place
I'm empty. I appreciate You for everything You
continually do for me, and for keeping me fully
supplied in every situation and need. I will look
to You when things look not enough.

Father, Your excellence is now! I believe today
will be filled with expressions of Your presence
and power, Your strength and peace, and Your
joy unspeakable! I thank You for loving me and
teaching me how to live by faith, with complete,
absolute trust in You, in Jesus' name. . .

SOMETIMES. . . we don't realize the depth and intensity of the struggle we've been in. It's so hard out there! We BE tired! We faced the trauma of the drama, the mountain that did not move, and the battle without spoils. We did it all with little, or mostly no support, breathing hard, determined to believe God, fighting off haters in hi-heeled hopes, and ducking fiery darts.

No breaks, no vacation, no time for R & R, and no recuperation of any losses! Please let's mention our frustration with so great a mistreatment while being misunderstood. We're way past busy and too worn out, with no understanding as to why it's too hot in the room where we've gotta serve mean, weird, ungrateful people who make your eyes hurt.

But God says, "STOP, in the name of love, being ashamed of being tired and empty." It's time to stop being embarrassed to be battle weary and up against all hope without a rope-a-dope move. We *must* stop the shame of running fully on empty.

Take off the cape! It's time to rest in the love of the Lord. It's time to remember who we are *to* God, Who is not a task master or slave runner. The test is over, and we passed it!

Like they did for Jesus in the wilderness (Mark 1:13), angels have come to minister refreshing to a weary, but wonderful people of God. Our atmosphere becomes Heaven's peace! We get restored by God's grace and our faith in Him!

SOME PEOPLE. . . will not be pleased with a better you, a healthier you, a wealthier you, a wiser, more-into-God and changed you. It's too bad they're still where you used to be! So, in the name of Jesus, keep moving, and pray for 'em!

SOME PEOPLE. . . think that other people are supposed to do for them what they should be doing for themselves. It's a failure to understand the need to develop the ability of right response, or, to have a response ability.

No one can help or fix someone who doesn't want to help or fix themselves. Continuing to sow in that field is a total waste of resources, energy, and precious time. It could also be considered a misplaced compassion. We all must take responsibility to develop a right response ability for ourselves, for our lives, and for our own personal issues and endeavors.

The Good News is God is available to us all! His mercies and graces are for any and every whosoever willing to avail them. Galatians 6:4-5 confirms: Let each one test his own work, then his reason to boast will be in himself alone, and not in his neighbor. For each will have to bear his own load.

SOME PEOPLE. . . have very interesting 'I' moments that, unfortunately, produce 'them' consequences!

SOME THOUGHTS. . .

Forget about being impressive. Be very concerned with being effective, which produces far reaching, impressive results.

Relationship with God can cause temptation to burn up before it manifests into a well attended distraction.

Laughter is the medicine to heal us from our tears and sorrow.

Be teachable, ready to hear, open to understand, and zealous to discover fresh, new revelation.

Never omit portions of God's Word, like items on a menu, that you're averse to, disagree with, or just don't want to heed. Only faith in and faithfulness to the Word release its full power, and the spiritual dynamics needed to fuel your life and purpose.

Nobody can tell you how to do something really great like the one who couldn't, and then could.

Don't be afraid to ask God for more. He has everything, owns it all, and He never runs out.

I DECLARE. . . I have an excellent spirit because God,
Who dwells within me, is excellence.

PROVERBS 8:11 ~ Wisdom is better than rubies, and all the
things one may desire cannot be compared with it.

NOTES & OBSERVATIONS. . .

_____

_____

_____

_____

_____

_____

_____

_____

_____

_____

_____

_____

_____

_____

DAY 24

GOD Is Love, Truth, Faithfulness, And Peace.

Teach me Your way, LORD, that I may rely
on Your faithfulness. Give me an undivided
heart, that I may fear Your name.

Psalm 86:11

PRAYER: My Jesus, on my own, what can
I do? Help me, because I have no answers.
Show me how to walk in Your way of doing,
and to do so in love, in spirit, and in truth.

Speak to my heart, Lord, more and more so
that I know to rely on Your faithfulness in my
every life situation. I'll trust You as I grow to
trust myself. Stand up within me so I will not
fail to become more like You. Father, please
keep me strengthened with courage to hold
onto You. My gratitude overflows to You and
Your every consideration! O my Lord, here's
my heart, in Jesus' name. . .

SOMETIMES. . . our questions turn to doubt. In Luke 7 is a powerful example. It's the story of an imprisoned John the Baptist sending a question to Jesus by messenger. Prior to his query, he had been sure about Jesus, his cousin. But in the grievous circumstances landing him in jail, with a death sentence, he began to question that certainty.

He knew personally Who Jesus was. He was a witness himself, seeing and hearing God, the Father, proclaiming, "This is My beloved Son in Whom I am well pleased" (Matthew 3:17). John didn't stop believing, but he wasn't as sure, as definite, as he was before. His situation wasn't encouraging. It gravely challenged him, as most great challenges do.

There is a difference between doubt and unbelief. Doubt may cause one to waiver between two or more opinions, while unbelief refuses to allow the acceptance of any truth, opinion or fact about the issue. Doubt makes us critical of God, but unbelief recoils our faith, and shuts God out.

Luke 7:19 shares John's question, "Are You the One?". In the midst of his personal madness, he lost his sure footing and remembrance of the many amazing things that transpired prior to his chains. Was his offense being reduced to the silent insignificance of his unheard voice? Or, was it the imminent 'soon' of not having a life that shook his soul to doubt?

The answer Jesus sent, "Blessed is he who is not offended because of Me," perhaps became John's conviction, his return to his senses, and, as well, his cooling board.

We often doubt when our faith is questioned in a way that is life threatening, or confronting to our identity or position. It's then we may forget God can answer questions we can't. He knows the weakness despair wreaks in our soul, and the human frailty we have to cope with in life, in crisis, or in the midnight hour of our chaos. He knows the full measure of our frame, yet He will never frame us with any shame.

God listens to hear our voice cry out to Him, whether we're in faith or doubt, in fear or unbelief, or in the worst mess of our lives. He listens, longing to help and extend to us the comfort, peace, and gracious mercies we need and call for. Whatever the climate of our condition, other than God to Whom we belong, our only need is faith in Him to willingly hear to save us. Because we call on His name, He answers (Acts 2:21).

Whenever doubt or unbelief dares invade, and before we panic in fear, *if* we place our faith in God, His faithfulness informs us that victory belongs to us! It's right on the other side of our call, our shout out to God, Who is our unfailing, always Savior, Father, and the Lover of our souls. Yes, we CAN trust Jesus! He is so sweet, and He is forever our Answer!

SOME PEOPLE. . . are bothered by our brokenness. Maybe it reminds them of their own. Maybe they view brokenness as a disability to one's function, value, or purpose. But in life, everybody has had to face some cracks. Some have stumbled on cracks, and some have suffered from crack.

We all fall short of any superiority. We're all vulnerable to fractures, physically or emotionally, and may have bits of remaining shrapnel, debris, crutches or chards from our past shatterings. The competition of who's had the worst woundings from the most maligned past seems sophomoric, but is sadly, disgustingly, a much too prevalent occurrence.

A fracture, or brokenness, doesn't automatically mean a dysfunction. God's destiny for us is not altered by any defect within us. No brokenness we suffer will prevent His blessings, cancel our call to purpose, or minimize our worth. God sealed our destiny *in Him*. It's part of His life plan devised out of His pure love for us, which is never seasonal, nor does it ever exit. His love and plan are as sure as He is forever God.

Whatever *happened to us* will not cast us from Him. A lisp or a limp, a lost identity or a fatty liver, we've got God Who makes things work together synergistically for our good and His glory. His all-knowingness knew us way before we knew Him!

God factored in every fracture, failing, fault, and every not-so-fun moment pertaining to our entire existence. He knew and saw our substance before its formation, and sorted out all our days while there were yet none of them (Psalm 139:16).

Our life is His doing and is doable because of what Jesus did for us, sacrificing His life for our salvation, AKA our whole life's rescue! We are recipients of the benefits of Christ's mission to replace our brokenness, cracks and all, with His radical loving grace of incomparable wholeness. And that's not all!

Along with that comes a transforming of our minds through the vehicle of conversating (praying) with Him, and what He's spoken to us in His Word, that Bible! The exchange is an infusion of healing - sealing up all our fragmented, inoperable parts and potential with His own power, strengths, character, and traits. It is quite mind boggling, but miraculous is a better word.

This great God Guy makes it personal. His love isn't a blanket statement, a generality to the masses. It is an individual, just for you affection, uniquely specific to each one of us, as only a good, perfect Father could give Himself to. He re-members us, so lovingly, from the rubble of our fragmentations.

We'll grow to know, by heart, His genteel, tender touch melting away the pains of shame, and loosing the chains to memories of our every debilitative breaking. What a love! What a God!

SOME THOUGHTS. . .

Comparisons destroy contentment, security and confidence.
Unless you're shopping for the best deal, or a better detergent,
abandon the proclivity to compare.

There are no blurred lines between the Kingdom of Light,
and the kingdom of darkness.

If we quit, we cannot experience continual, progressive growth
in our processing to breakthrough.
Quitting is not the same as leaving which, in some instances,
may be a necessary action of resolve.
But, you must leave whatever makes you quit becoming you.

Distractions are detours that deviate from your life's direction.

What do you do when your circumstances don't quite match
what God has spoken? PRAY, BELIEVE, TRUST, PRAISE,
THANK GOD, WORSHIP, ADJUST YOUR SIGHTS, REPEAT!

You are most prudent, productive and effective when you are
appreciated. Always avoid being tolerated.

I DECLARE. . . Today I accept the responsibility to grow and prosper by yielding to the will and power of God.

PSALM 119:34 ~ Give me understanding, and I shall keep Your law. Indeed, I shall observe it with my whole heart.

NOTES & OBSERVATIONS. . .

_____

_____

_____

_____

_____

_____

_____

_____

_____

_____

_____

_____

_____

_____

DAY 25

GOD Is No Respecter Of Persons. Whatever He's Done For Anyone, He Will Do For You.

You must be completely faithful to the LORD.
Worship and obey only the LORD and do
this with fear and trembling.
Deuteronomy 13:4

PRAYER: O God, please teach me to know Your will concerning every matter of my life, and help me yield to it. Your understanding and wisdom are the help and graces I need to obey Your commands. I am available, my Father, by my own volition and desire.

Thank You, Lord, for holding onto me when I get weak, for shoring me up when I'm torn by doubts, stress, fears or weakness. Draw me closer to You. Give me grace to fall into Your arms of love and mercy, even now, in the blessed name of Jesus. . .

SOMETIMES. . . our knowledge and understanding of God are way too small, and hinder to minimize our faith. To know the God we don't know very well yet, we need to get closer to Him, leaning on Him, not our understanding (Proverbs 3:5) or knowledge, and accepting His terms of engagement.

Being open to get more God is a beautiful journey, almost like courtship. But it can be scary at the same time if we hold too tightly to what we know and understand. To find God, we need God, and an earnest effort of pursuit, with all abandonment of any personal agenda, experience or religious mindset.

In that pursuit, we may get fired up with passion after what we want and think we need, but we don't always pursue, with the same flame, what we really need - relationship with God. Is it, 'Yes, Father in Heaven!', or, 'Yay, Heavenly Concierge!'?

Seeking God for Himself may be a new thing, not having been consistently a first thing priority (Matthew 6:33). But, by God's mercy, and as long as we're still breathing, it's not too late to come closer to God Who's been waiting the whole time to be closer to us! Isaiah 30:18 confirms His heart's desire: The Lord waits, longing to be gracious to you... that He may have mercy on you and show lovingkindness to you... Blessed are all those who wait for Him, who *expect, look and long for Him!*

God waits! That's rich! And in the process, in the wait, He is gradually growing us, drawing us closer to Him, His love and ways, His mind and understanding, bypassing our full-of-self thinking. He waits for us to come out of our assumptions, error, ideas, and inadequate information, to arrive at a tenderness to His truth, which is one of His names. Coming to know Him as such introduces us to a form of 'free' we have never tasted or known, let alone lived or imagined. (John 8:32).

While God waits, He never contemplates leaving, reviling, or rejecting us. He's always drawing us to Himself, to *know* Him and His person. What an outrageously inexorable consideration! We need only to open our eyes, our heart, our mind and our hands to grasp onto His exceeding greatness, His abundantly more everything. Imagine - God, and His Almightyness, we can actually behold, have, experience and know. WHAT!!!

God loves us diligently seeking Him for He waits, wanting to reward us with graces to grow up our faith and our life in Him. These terms of His endearment are incentives and benefits of relationship with Him! Why wait to expand the territories of our life, faith, purpose, and by far, the greatest blessing - an amazing connect to God? It's time to know Him personally, and very well! That's big, and the greatest of all relationships ever! So, please, fa'get about religion, and all other lesser things.

SOME PEOPLE. . . are folk who can be counted on, and some are folk to be counted out. The rule is to *never* take either one personal to avoid any animus in the mix.

We're called to be interdependent on each other, and fully dependent on God. But when we avail to certain situations, others may not, despite agreeing to do so. It's simply a tutorial to *always trust God first.* For in all things, we can count on Him Who is faithful, and will not fail or bail. When challenges, upsets or disappointments confront, trust God to work all things out, and always for our best interest (Romans 8:28).

SOME PEOPLE. . . don't grow with you so they can't continue to go with you. They may be really nice people, but if no deposits toward your purpose show up from them, it's a clue to detach from cords of limitation and deficiency.

Being friendly is good and less costly than the demanding loyalty of highly engaged, unproductive so-called friendships. Adjusting can take time, and isn't always easy, but God prunes with precise, timely and appropriate cuts.

God does not want us in bondage to anyone jes' for them or their sake, their happiness, or relational handicaps. We are His first and before we belong to anybody or anything. It's a blessing to remember: Freedom, purpose, and you are priceless!

SOME THOUGHTS. . .

The ultimate act of love is to love those who don't and won't love you in return. That's what Jesus did and always does.

What you consider, you open your heart to.
Will you consider the Promises of God, or will you only consider the problems you face?

Within your purpose is the help, solution and answer to someone else's problem.

God's Faves: You, your faith, your worship and obedience.

All things may not work together for those who are called to purpose but decline to answer, who remain out of order, who stay out of service, and who are totally self-consumed.

If we refuse to be impressed by what we can do, we won't be depressed by what we can't do.

Serve God with all you have, and He will give you everything you need, and a bunch of stuff you want.

I DECLARE. . . I am forever grateful to God because His goodness and mercy pursue and find me!

JEREMIAH 15:21 ~ I will deliver you from the hand of the wicked, and I will redeem you from the grip of the terrible.

NOTES & OBSERVATIONS. . .

_____

_____

_____

_____

_____

_____

_____

_____

_____

_____

_____

_____

_____

_____

DAY 26

GOD's Workings Will Not Be
Hindered Or Reversed.

Listen to advice and accept instruction,
that you may gain wisdom in the future.
Many are the plans in a man's mind but
it is the LORD's purpose that will stand.
Proverbs 19:20-21

PRAYER: Lord, today I'm asking You for
the wisdom and strategies to accomplish
my purpose. Your guidance and counsel,
Father, will lead me toward that end.

I thank You, God, for giving me the right
tools in my arsenal. I thank You for favor,
divine connections and open doors, and
Your perfect timing to walk through them
with clear perspective. Help me see 'the'
door of Your appointment for me without
fear or intimidation, but with humility and
gratitude. In Jesus' name I pray. . .

SOMETIMES. . . we have to bear one another's burdens, as in, be a help. At the same time, we're each responsible for carrying our own load (Galatians 6:2, 4-5). The idea is to have some compassion without any fret of being taken advantage of, or any threat of being dealt a hand of guilt.

We've all got friends who ask for an assist from time to time. We lend a hand if we're good to do so, even when it may not be a convenient add-on to our calendar. If the same friends are the always 'help me out' callers, discernment has to clock in. Determining whether or not we've changed roles from the 'ol' friend' to 'the help', AKA the enabler, is required. Enabling roles enable them, in their role, to be nervy users of friends, and the remainders of negligent irresponsibility.

Sooner or later, in the case of the latter, we must realize 'No!' is a real, complete sentence. Great big explanations are a no-no, but truth is to be said in love. Perhaps the 'No!' will be the needed wake up call for those who always call for help, and the answer to end some calls to the called on.

God helps us, and He wants to help them, relieving us of cape duty. We must be wise stewards of all we have and give, as in us, our time, treasure or talents. Beautiful boundaries come in knowing the when of 'no', and the when of 'yes', speaking both in love, for God's glory, and for remaining free and friends!

SOME PEOPLE. . . have no spiritual hunger. They don't want to be empowered spiritually any more than folk with no appetite want to be fed. Like a parked car, they're going nowhere and are quite happy with their still life lifestyle.

Somewhere in the history of their chosen inanimation, it could be that something or someone shifted their gears to a neutral position, or the off duty of a parking space. Earlier on, maybe real rebuttal roused from their lips, but now, it's crickets, with no budging them from this muted mindset.

What is the 'it' keeping them so still, so stayed spiritually? With a bit of a prod, they often and adamantly utter the ol', half-truth excuse of 'me and God, we're just fine!'. That's all the 'splainin' offered. There are no smiles or frowns (Is it Botox?).

But don't worry or fret! In an effort to crack their case, pray and entrust them to God, for prayers avail much. In His timing, they will hunger, thirst and need to taste and see His goodness. Be salty, stay lit, and remember, is anything too hard for God?

SOME PEOPLE. . . deem their actions as unseen, forgetting God sees absolutely everything! Whatever is unlike Him is not only seen, but may get a lil' smelly since the fragrance of the knowledge of God has gone missing. So then, what is seen, or unseen, can be fragrant, or not so much.

SOME THOUGHTS. . .

1 Samuel 16:1-13 is the story of the Prophet Samuel going to the house of Jesse to anoint one of his sons king of Israel. It was a challenge because the Lord did not reveal which son it would be. Judging by the looks of the seven sons present in the house, the Prophet assumed he knew just which one. But, it was none who were there.

The youngest son, David, was out in the fields tending sheep. He wasn't asked to come in because he was not considered by his own father. David, like many of us, may not have been considered, accepted or included by his father, or other folk, but he was chosen by God, and set apart for purpose.

What problem would it have been if Dave had been allowed in the room? Those who are left out, excluded by the world, family members, and even by the holy folk in church, shall be the ones God uses and calls for His plans and purposes.

Invisibility is not a symptom of insignificance. David wasn't forgotten, he was hidden by God. What is precious and invaluable is always set apart and kept hidden from commonality.

Never waste time and energy *trying* to be seen and accepted. God sees you, loves you, and He's called and purposed you. Allow His great love for you to be your focus and spot light!

I DECLARE. . . I will walk in the Spirit of God, Who will, therefore, affect everything I do.

PSALM 119:93 ~ I will never forget Your precepts, for by them You have given me life.

NOTES & OBSERVATIONS. . .

DAY 27

GOD Alone Is The Lord! There Was No Other
God Before Him Nor Will There Be After Him.

You shall love the LORD your God with all
your heart, with all your soul,
and with all your mind.
Deuteronomy 6:5, Matthew 22:37

PRAYER: Lord, You are the Lover of my
soul, the Knower of my heart. I love You,
God. I thank You for loving me. I want to
know all Your heart and mind!

Lord, show me how to connect others to
You. I desire to reach outside myself, my
own understanding, to know the need for
You in others. I want compassion to walk
in love without offense toward those who
offend. Help me to forgive and love those
who are a challenge to love. Grow me to
do this for You, Lord, and for Your glory,
in Jesus Christ's name. . .

SOMETIMES. . . you just have to leave.
It's the only way you can come back better.

SOMETIMES. . . our relationships with certain folk were just to get them to Jesus. Whereas, some relationships with other folk, good and bad, were just to get us to Jesus.

SOMETIMES. . . we need to stretch! S-T-R-E-T-C-H past the security of ourselves and what we know, and the insecurity of our inadequacies and what we don't know yet.

We need to stretch to reach for dependence on God alone to help us align our lives with Him, and to harmonize our soul - our mind, will and emotions, with His will.

We need to stretch toward fresh and new, where we have no frame of reference, in order to take our focus off the familiar - the 'where' we've been for way too long.

SOMETIMES. . . God won't meet our needs-based prayer requests not to disappoint us, but to exceed them. When we ask too small, we forget He is God, the Great God, Who loves us madly, Who is a crazy good and amazing Parent, Who is faithful to care for us, and Who owns everything!

SOME PEOPLE. . . need help. Others need prayer! And prayer can be the uber to all the help we need.

Prayer is a grand grace of power and authority! It's the gift of communication with God. Prayer allows us to conversate with God! It's a cleverness of God to bring us close to Himself.

Prayer can present a moment to tell God all about how hard it is, who did what, why we're mad and up all hours of the night, and to ask what ever happened to His promised relief checks. Somehow, in our bent knee and bowed body posture, we don't recall He already knows all about our troubles. He's very woke and aware of our grief and grievances (Isaiah 53:3).

Interestingly enough, God will allow trouble, issues and needs to crash our party to get us to phone Home. He lets us sink jes' low enough for our need for Him to rise up. It's then He begins to lift us up higher, and out of the mire (Psalm 40:2).

A beautiful facet of prayer, it turns us toward God. The saying 'prayer changes things' is truth. The first thing changed is us, because prayer is purposed to kill our will, a huge benefit that helps us surrender our oft swoll-up-with-pride flesh! It's a humbler, and at the same time a privilege, to ask God for His help. God, Who is all the help we will ever need, by His Divine Love Plan, made us to be His children, fully dependent on Him!

Through our prayer conversations, God graces us to see and know ourselves and the issues, faced or denied, that keep us *in* our dysfunctions, lack of knowledge, and our recurring, anti-purpose disorders. The more we pray, the more we'll grow to know Him as a Father, Counsellor, Friend and Confidant. The more we pray, the more we'll understand our trust in Him is considered greatly by God, because it is sacred to God.

We'd do well to pray without ceasing (1 Thessalonians 5:17), as in regularly, daily, the thing to do particularly prior to doing anything of importance. God gave this precious gift to nurture and connect us to Him in an unbreakable fellowship. Prayers for our needs are heard, but relational, close, pillow-talk type, intimately spoken words become priority when we know Who we are talking to. It's like an all access, backstage pass.

Relationship with God will bring our shoulders down from our ears when they get raised by the distractions of fear, offense, doubts, or frustration. God's comforting words of promise are medication for our soul's peace, and an invitation to know His love and faithfulness to answer us. Our prayers invite Him to: *Prevail* over us and our issues; *Provide* for us in all aspects of our life; *Produce* progress, increase, and growth everywhere we are; *Prevent* what we can't; and *Protect* us in all we do!

At the beginning and at the end of every day, PRAY PEOPLE!

SOME THOUGHTS. . .

Psalm 34:1 I will bless the Lord at all times! His praise shall
      continually be in my mouth. As well it should!
How can we not praise God and thank Him for all He's done
for us, even up to this very moment? THINK: How many times
has God kept you from near misses, seen or unseen dangers,
sick people you got too close to, getting hurt by an almost, kinda, sorta relationship, or the consequences of unwise, or just
dumb decisions? We too easily don't remember His graces!

With all that, we're still breathing and going to work on a job
God provided. We're getting dressed without a caregiver, duly
functioning in all our capacities, and eating meals in a place
with a roof, a bed, and food in the fridge, jes' to name a few.

Despite the haters and inclement weather, somebody actually
said and meant, 'Good Morning'! It's ALL good, it's ALL God.
It's a joy and privilege to praise Him from Whom all blessings
flow unceasingly, with or without our asks or thanks!

God always delivers, and far more frequently than Domino's.
He sees to it we arrive on time with the power and anointing
to be fully equipped for the assignment, purposefully appointed, profoundly effective, with extra pepperoni, if we want it!

I DECLARE. . . My commitment to God is without any options to stop, quit, compromise, or turn back.

JEREMIAH 29:13 ~ You will seek Me and find Me, when you search for Me with all your heart.

NOTES & OBSERVATIONS. . .

DAY 28

GOD, The LORD, Makes A Way Out Of No Way.

I tell you the truth, anyone who has faith in
Me will do what I have been doing. He
will do even greater things than these
because I am going to the Father.

John 14:12

PRAYER: Lord, I thank You for the grace of
faith in You! Thank You for considering me to
be set apart, chosen, called to Your purpose.
I am truly privileged to lift up the name Jesus
to those You cause me to encounter.

Your trust is precious to me. I am grateful for
Your Holy Spirit power within me making me
effectively alive for You. God, be seen in me!
Bless me to be a real blessing to others, and
an honor to You, for Your Kingdom and Your
name sake. I believe in You! Hear my prayer
in Jesus' wonderful name. . .

SOMETIMES. . . brokenness, in spirit and in heart, can be worn as a badge, as a woe-is-me mindset. People get frauded into thinking they are the exception to God's love and life.

Being crushed and wounded continually can hinder our faith walk and our service to God. Because it's not consistent with any Bible lifestyle, brokenness can become a learned behavior and a detriment. It gets passed on, like contamination, to others and future generations. To that end, the enemy uses unhealed areas of our lives to continue to crush, pervert and enslave. The lie is the 'broken' are unfit, unworthy, and those who will never be normal, healed, or used by God.

God doesn't erase nor etch-a-sketch our memories. But He is able to heal us from our past's pain, and make our story a testimony for others who've been hurt and broken in heart. Truly, healing and deliverance are *choices* - deliberate decisions to change our lives, the past's effects, or the current conditions.

We're not made to cope with difficulty! We are to confront any and all unlike God issues. It's our choice to be free from whatever imposes captivity, harm or illegal incarceration!

God made us to receive every thing Jesus' brokenness gifted us! They belong to us for we belong to God. We are indeed healed, whole, set free, fully alive and well (John 8:36)!

SOME PEOPLE. . . define and limit you to how they met you. Their judgments frame you into their visual assessment of the initial counter without knowing you at all.

There's no consideration for an 'un' season when unhealthy judgments land. That meet-up day just happened to be your down day, the day you weren't so shiny, the day you sang a bit off key on your solo, the day you got messed up, messed with, and messaged the wrong text. It's the day you didn't get your hair done, making you undone on jes' one of those days.

Rather than react to their insensitivity, as if that day was your whole life, simply remember who you are, O child of God - a person of purpose! Coming to your senses about *you*, usually displaces you from disgruntled folk whose task it is to misdefine anyone not exactly like them. They suffer discomfort over you getting out and over all the crazies that led to the doleful disarray displayed on 'that' day, in the first dang place!

Being a displaced person of purpose, O God child, means you won't fit in, and you can't. Truth is, you're in this world but not of it. That truth pours out this wisdom: Wrong perceptions are fraudulent critiques that disconnect people, stifle possibilities, and are contraries to purpose. But there's a grace in being displaced! It's *the help* in taking no offense, and *the gift* in taking time to pray for folk needing *the God* Who is in loving people!

SOME THOUGHTS. . .

Note To Self: Just going to church won't develop relationship with God any more than reading about spaceships and the solar system will make you an astronaut.

We cannot function secularly and grow spiritually.

Sin is the only merchandise we purchase without looking, even once, at the price tag.

Faith keeps us moving out of the chaos, out of the flood, out of the pit, out of the den of lions, and out of our wildernesses. Faith moves us forward, forbidding our stay in places which are less than God's victory and purpose for us.

The places we move to are required classrooms that teach us, and impart to us experiential knowledge of faith in God. Each place holds light to truths of the vast, magnitudinal greatness of His love and power, intention and faithfulness. From these apprisings we are commenced and commissioned with a new depth of substantive, personal revelation, and an irrefutable, confirming, proving confession of evidence!

Deception reigns when we believe a lie, or disbelieve the truth.

I DECLARE. . . I thank God for answering my prayers and
always exceeding my expectations.

JOB 22:21 ~ Acquaint yourself with God, and be at peace,
thereby good will come to you.

NOTES & OBSERVATIONS. . .

_____

_____

_____

_____

_____

_____

_____

_____

_____

_____

_____

_____

_____

_____

_____

DAY 29

*GOD Blots Out Our Mistakes And Stumblings,
And Does Not Remember Our Sins.*

Know this, my beloved brothers, let every
person be quick to hear, slow to speak,
slow to anger, for man's anger does
not produce the righteousness of God.
James 1:19-20

PRAYER: My God, You know my thoughts
afar off. I need Your mind and Your Spirit to
be imparted for my renewal. I thank You for
Your tender mercies drawing me to the right
attitudes of my heart and soul.

Lord, I give You my reins to direct my mind
toward Your way of thinking, which is higher
than my own thoughts, ideas or imaginings.
Thank You for loving me enough to change
me for my better good, and for Your glory. I
yield to Your will, in Jesus' holy name. . .

SOMETIMES. . . what we're hearing, or what we've heard, brings fear on our street, onto the driveway, right up the steps to our lives, and ringing the doorbell.

This fear assignment, a pit maneuver, has come to drown out God's voice speaking to us, to our life, and to what we see. So hearing is not only sound, but a carrier of in-depth, hi-def, visual perception. Selah that for a moment!

When we hear a word, like 'apple', we see the word. What we hear transmits a pictorial projection which can also prompt corresponding actions and responses.

Like a domino effect, what lands in our ear gate can manifest in our lives. Romans 10:17 says, faith comes by hearing what is spoken or preached of the Word of God. In the same way, fear, stress or anxiety, come by hearing what is spoken in lies, misinformation, opinions, or other fraud born images. Faith, or fear, gets formed, and cast for viewing into our minds.

Any weakness in the mind gets changed to strength by our deliberate choice to be mindful of what God speaks in His Word, the only transformer of our mind (Romans 12:2). It's so clever of God, the Manufacturer of the mind, to give instruction for its use, health and function. Following His tutorials, to the full, will build up our faith, our person, and how we function in our lives.

Therefore, our deliberate and wise choices direct us to walk through the door of change into stability, instead of fear. We get transformed, by our yes to faith, into *what God says* to us, about us, and about all things pertaining to us.

Colossians 3:16 Let the Word of Christ, the Message, have the run of the house. Give it plenty of room in your lives...
using good common sense. O Selah!
John 15:7 But if you make yourselves at home with Me and My words are at home in you, you can be sure that whatever you ask will be listened to and acted upon.

God's Word and His words to us, if taught, studied and heard, will transform our mind not only to hear what He says, but to see His intentionality in all He speaks. This gives great reason to align ourselves with God, as in obey and agree, yielding to Him in every other area of our lives and concerns.

In this privileged invite to synchronicity with God, He's saying He hears *what we speak*, reminding us we also cast visions with our words. What He hears us say, by our faith in Him and His Word, He will make manifest to be visibly seen!

We must *say what He says*! He promises to produce His Word spoken. We'll see them show up as peace and power, as what no eye has seen and no ear has heard, like apples of gold, on our street, walking through the door, landing grace in our face!

SOME PEOPLE. . . hold fast to their 'way of faith'. It's non-denominational, bapti-costal, method-tarian, or church of me and God. Their personal dogma determines their reality, their faith produce, and the future outcome of their purpose.

Upbringing, prior religious doctrine or training, positive and negative life experiences, culture, what did or didn't happen, ad infinitum, are contributing criteria for their faith's basis. All these components can systematically affect their heart and soul to the point of taking control, and influence not only elements of the heart and soul, but also their life and purpose.

The personal go-to's of such a 'creative' approach to God can acutely infiltrate thoughts, imaginations and lifestyle. However innocently formed, some become a sordid stronghold of error, and religious, even cultish, dictates. If not founded in God and valid doctrine, non-Word based beliefs can becloud believers, defining and limiting their entire life, as well as override truth because of their long standing preeminence.

Examine your beliefs at the core. Are they founded and seated in God and His Word? Do they allow Him to be the Lord, in Whom you truly believe, and the Center of your life? Or, are they brazenly at the helm, directing your life's course, manning your heart and soul's control center, isolating and steering you away from God's will and plan for your destiny? Uh... SELAH!

SOME THOUGHTS...

Forward and ahead - though unfamiliar and foreign, are where peace, growth, favor, new, and blessings live.

Always maintain a safe-for-you environment.

Count all your blessings, thanking God for the great ones and the small, including even the least of them.

A plateau is a semi-promised land state of being, or a respite. It's an interim blessing to accommodate seasons of growth, prior to the building up to a newer platform. It's as a temporary harbor, a soft place of landing, for assessment and adjustment.

God blesses us in our hiatus time. Though He never plateaus, He allows us this grace to transition, refresh, and recover, to catch our breath, reignite, and prepare to move forward.

As only a loving Father could, God knows our frame, and our need of adjustments. Hence, His grace of plateau to level off just before we matrix through to our next level of excellence. Breathe deep. Rock steady. Better is about to BE!

You can't put on Christ and you at the same time.

I DECLARE. . . Today I will represent Jesus in everything I do.

JEREMIAH 33:3 ~ Call on Me and I will answer you. I'll tell you

marvelous and wondrous things that you could

never figure out on your own.

NOTES & OBSERVATIONS. . .

_____

_____

_____

_____

_____

_____

_____

_____

_____

_____

_____

_____

_____

_____

DAY 30

GOD Alone Is Savior!
Besides Him There Is No Savior.

In righteousness you shall be established.
You shall be far from oppression, for
you shall not fear, and from terror,
for it shall not come near you.

Isaiah 54:14

PRAYER: God, You bless me far beyond
my comprehension. You keep me, protect
me, and give me victory over every battle.
Lord Jesus, my thanks and praise, my life
and love, my whole heart belong to You.

When I rise, You are there. Wherever I am
throughout my day, You are there. If I don't
know the way, You always find me, helping
me to stand sure. O Father, I worship You!
Please give me the capacity to have more
of You. I ask in Jesus' name. . .

SOMETIMES. . . it's difficult! It's seldom easy. Whether it's the external taunts of the world, the people and the issues, or the internal haunts within the heart, the home and the personals, difficult times barge in to confront, interrupt, and annoy.

Adversity, their real name, can yank us down into devastating trauma, and then begin to stalk us with unsettling desperation, unleashing an emotional hot mess. Stunned, visiting the state of shock, we become almost muted in amazement.

Stellar acting in the play of adversity can be performed by our very cool decision to declare lines of truth. Note, adversity is not an insurmountable, surround-sound wall. It's a big, fat test to be successfully passed and turned into a stepping stone up over its clutter and confusion wrought crazies. To see difficulty morph into a handrail forward is to see God in the mix.

As the dust from all that debris begins to settle, we clearly get it: We got rescued, saved again, from an intended destruction, by His grace! Even the stain of the pain turns to a fade when shouts of praise fall from our awestruck lips. Praise is a choice and a wise decision! It is our follow up to God's super cool response to our premeditated reach for His strong arm.

In adversity's big show, acting responsibly is our power line of truth. It's real maturity to grasp sooner than later in order to be deftly prepared to resist opposition to God's promised real life.

For if we're not disciplined to prepare, our rescue from adversity is, at best, a temporary fix of a chronic condition that continually appears again and again, and always too soon.

As much as adversity is relentless, our press against it ought to have consistently persistent scenes and schemes of intolerance to its oppression. Our intentioned, deliberate choice must be to finish well, standing strong against every conflicting wind we face, and to posture yet another line of truth.

Jesus champs us up in John 16:33, "These things I have spoken to you, that in Me you may have peace. In the world *you will have tribulation*; but be of good cheer, I have overcome the world." The Amplified adds, "I have deprived it of the power to harm you and have conquered it *for you*." Wows!

In this line of truth, God blasts His desire to show up where we live, work, get challenged, and in the impossibilities of our adversity. WHO is like Him Who cares for folk who may or may not show up to say 'thanks!'? He's not like us, in that we'd be inconsolably crying in all the disregard. But He is like us, in the fact He identified with us, becoming acquainted with *all* of our griefs, sorrows, and human vulnerabilities (Hebrews 4:15).

Somehow He loves us unconditionally, and He likes us, too! Because He does, He overcame everything to overcome what is too dang hard for us. What a good Guy! What a great God!

SOME PEOPLE. . . still only see men as trees. They don't, won't, or can't see clearly. Even after God's been working on them and with them, sending His 'peeps' to them armed with a word and oil, there's no change. Faithful to heal on a regular basis, God waits in their still-don't-see-ness.

The problem, more often than not, is they cannot admit they don't have it all together. This issue is their ammo to keep on criticizing petulantly, aiming to be hard on others who have a few blind spots. They refuse to acknowledge their own low vision while they deny their inability to see clearly. Owning up to one's inadequacies is a right, but a truth pride won't allow.

Being right is not a right. What is right is admitting our human frailties, faults, and failings. It takes great courage to see past the need to be right, and to rejoice over the truth that Jesus calls us ALL righteous knowing we're ALL far from it.

To receive such clarifying truth requires a teachable spirit, and a real 'want to'. With this combo plate, we'll get to see, at last! We can thank God Almighty we will clearly see, at last!

The Lessons: #1. We are not called to have it all together, but to altogether believe and love God Who's great at healing our eyes and all else. #2. A commitment to sight is *wanting* new eyes to see like God sees - clearly, correctly, in depth, in full, beyond ourselves, and all of that on a regular basis.

SOME THOUGHTS. . .

Hold fast, stay focused, keep moving, press on - you are
closer now than when you first believed.

Another reason to praise God: WHO else can you call all day,
all night, anytime, every time, always, constantly, 24/7, 365
days of every year, and always get an answer?

Be sober and never intoxicated with misinformation, anxiety,
fake news, stress, social media, adversity, offenses, or the
cares and the cra-cra people of this world.

When what's in front of you becomes more important than
what's behind you, you will always find a way to proceed.

You've got nothing to prove and only One to please.
Cancel all the auditions, and stop trying out for the position
God has already made you for.
Your anointing is God saying you've been pre-approved.

The greatest life worth living starts with dying to the flesh,
and every 'selfie', all about me, mentality.

I DECLARE. . . God's love for me is relentless! It never quits, never gives up, never ends, and never runs out.

2 SAMUEL 7:22a ~ You are great, O LORD God. For there is none like You, nor is there any God besides You.

NOTES & OBSERVATIONS. . .

_____

_____

_____

_____

_____

_____

_____

_____

_____

_____

_____

_____

_____

_____

_____

God's peace surpasses

your understanding, while it

mends your fragmented pieces.

4TH

QUARTER

DAY 31

GOD Is Unfailing In Mercy And Kindness.

O LORD, You are the great and awesome
God! You always fulfill Your promises
of unfailing love to those who love
You and keep Your commands.

Daniel 9:4

PRAYER: Jesus, keep me close to You!
Help me hear and recognize Your voice,
to know Your will and plans for me. Lead
me to follow You and Your directions well.

Father, thank You for grace to obey Your
commands, to honor You, and to commit
to pursue You in all my ways. I trust You,
Lord, with all my heart, for You humbled
Yourself to consider me. Help me live for
You, love You, and give my all to You, in
the power of Jesus' name. . .

SOMETIMES. . . God allows trouble to show up in your life to expose those who are *not for you*, only because He knows *when* you're ready to know, and *need* to know, who they are.

For God knows much of the divisiveness and deception of ill-intentions, disguised in the wraps of friendly, is staged to lure any conscionable or wise thinking right out of your mind. And as clever as enemies are, it's easy to be snared by traps leading to great disappointment when you're unsuspecting.

In the dance of deception, what was meant for your hurt, God turns for your good, all while you glide across that dance floor. It's just another reason not to reason, but to give God thanks!

Disappointment may lurk in the lure of disguise, but God will make His own to discern, and to be wise.

SOMETIMES. . . tears do the talking. It's good, alright, and very healthy to cry. Tears cleanse the soul of the toxins from living life, hurts and pain, wrongs imposed, consequences of bad choices, hardships, or loss of relationships.

Tears are unspoken prayers that water the garden path along our journey. God counts them, adding to them graces to heal us, comfort our soul, and grow us up and forward.

SOME PEOPLE. . . get infatuated with who they think they are because of what they've accomplished and their history of achievements. The same folk get dismayed over what hasn't been received yet, and what they can't quite do or get yet. Oh, the wait for the next big thing is pain!

The path they're on is dimly lit. They give no mind to appreciation, since recognition is their ultimate goal and only passion. It's all they ever talk about, think of, or anxiously live for.

But appreciation is knit to gratitude. Without gratitude for what we do have, appreciation will escape us altogether, as will any acknowledgement of God as the Giver of all things.

Mark 8:36 For what will it profit a man if he gains the whole world, and loses his own soul? Wise words for every people! To consider and receive such wisdom adds credibility to our life and faith walk. More words of weight, so worthy of consideration, tell us the whole earth, and all who live on the planet, belong to God (Psalm 24:1). HE is the sole Owner! Note well, nobody else is, though they may be in possession.

No matter what we acquire, have innately, or earn by way of labors, it all belongs to our Owner, God. By His generosity, He allows us to possess, or steward, whatever things we receive. For this we should forever say, "Thank You, God!"

SOME THOUGHTS. . .

Perspective is simply how you see things. It's essential to season and temper your perspective with wisdoms gleaned from your experiences, and those of others you trust. This enables you to distinguish well, with reasonable certainty and without unnecessary error, the choices and decisions you'll encounter to produce and make progress on the journey forward.

Perspective lends both understanding to matters of concern, and clarity to things worthy of your attention and efforts. Its insight vets well, preventing investments toward what is not prudent or relevant, nor stout with potential toward purpose.

A clear perspective keenly sees past what it looks like to what it could be, sensing a positive in difficulty, and an opportunity in crisis. Clear perspective knows right. It will grow when your eyes are on God because He increases your 'see' ability.

A personal perspective, without right focus, has the potential to shade the truth in life's realities, and be oblivious to discern the obvious. Right focus is urgent for proper perspective, and the only way to live above your natural see level.

Whatever your focus, attention to it gives it life. Right focus, developed by prayer and connectivity to God, is fixed to perpetually grow the expanse and life of clear perspective.

I DECLARE. . . Today, right now, anything that would attempt to terminate, limit, or thwart my progress will cease.

ACTS 2:28 ~ You have made known to me the paths of life. You will fill me with joy in Your presence.

NOTES & OBSERVATIONS. . .

DAY 32

GOD Blesses Us To Make Us A Blessing Forever.

> In my trouble, deep trouble, I prayed to God.
> He answered me. From the belly of the
> grave I cried, 'Help!' You heard my cry.
>
> *Jonah 2:2*

PRAYER: My God, my Father, You bless
me! O Lord, with You, everyday is greater
than the day before. How my soul rejoices
in Your countless generosities and beyond
kindnesses You constantly pour out on me.
I can't thank You enough for eyes that see,
ears that hear, and lips that praise You!

Dear Jesus, will You please help me be a
better blessing, more generous and kind?
Make me a distributor of You, a believable
displayer of Your beauty, love and power,
Your mercies and grace. I am asking in
Your great name, Jesus. . .

SOMETIMES. . . a shift causes a rift. The shift, an altered state, causes rippling wave effects in lots of areas previously not considered (surprise, surprise!) in the initial notion to step forward. Thus, the rift. Who knew?

It's not always easy to shift. As to the rift, its unplanned show up manifests as a split, or a shake up. The end result may be a breakup, often causing an abrupt alteration of associations, positions, directions, plans, and actions, plus!

Things and people are subject to fall away while other things and people are suddenly, strategically, moved toward you. Understand, separation is necessary since room must be made for add-ons or replacements. Like de-cluttering, it's a process to reconfigure space for something greater, bigger, newer, and better. The current ground of space shakes loose the unnecessary, the not new or current enough, and the unproductive, to accommodate the restructure for a new quality of order.

New wine is a shift. It causes a rift in the old wine skins. The rift breaks the skins to uselessness. There has to be a newer, better quality skin to contain the new, now wine!

The rift makes space for revision. It's purposed by God Who deems it necessary in His plan for your forward motion. The new space, the clearer, open venue is God ordained for the new order, which will break off everything unlike Him, in every and all places within you, your life, and your desires.

God's predestined plan for His people is to live alive, blessed and fruitful, and to produce and prosper. The configurations in the mind are often the old wines skins of dysfunction that God begins shifting to fall away. Like wheat's chaff that was once useful but now unnecessary, they fall away to be discarded.

God's new order necessitates division of the ordinary and extraordinary, the familiar and unfamiliar, the relevant and obsolete. It shifts you into new territories, making room for the new positions and capacities, the new opportunities and connections. It brings a brand new now to bloom!

With the bloom is found things and people, never imagined to be fallen away, distanced in the path behind. Within its unfolding, in the wake of the shift forward, is a new shade of future which seemed unattainable, and so very impossible. As it is a no frame of reference now, it is a for-the-first-time new.

Taking God's way out of the old into the new, you discover an inner freedom from running, scared, back to where you started. You don't need to find the right Letting Go speech, voicing the intended to detach, 'don't look back' narrative. Your new shift's task: Thank God, from Whom all blessings flow!

SOME PEOPLE. . . constantly reach for accomplishments, achievements, and acquisitions, not realizing, nor ever considering, none of these things are any part of who they really are. Acceptance, attention, and applause are sought after layers, the much desired attraction, of their savvy wardrobe. In their mind, they've got 'the look' they want known better!

These 'things' may be fabulous factions, très trendy, and astonishingly stellar treasures. However, at best, they merely accessorize one's life, like dangling earrings and stretch bracelets.

The glitz and the glam, the buzz and the notice, do well to produce popularity and applause. But regardless to how spectacularly they make rapture of the senses and emotions, they don't contribute any value to anybody's identity or worth.

Reaching only for what decorates, augments, or accompanies to enhance one's life is human effort full of empty calories. Any 'see-me' agenda is blind to God's pure light, the illumination of His loving heart of acceptance. To miss God dismisses all purpose, leaving appropriate attention askew. Without this grace-light, self-ness can darken every area of endeavor. Why disregard God, in Whose life we live, move, breathe, and are lit?

No one is as beautiful, stunning and attractive, as the one who God adorns with His Light, and robes in His Righteousness!

SOME THOUGHTS. . .

God reveals Himself to us on the level of our understanding and spiritual maturity, on the basis of our need to know, and on the premise of our desire after Him.

Five Directives For Good Success:

1. Vanquish every excuse for failure.

2. Never allow loyalty to replace competence.

3. Defy the facts, and always defect to the truth.

4. Have faith to receive more than you usually do.

5. Come out from among the limiters of your purpose.

Gratitude heals low vision, a preventer of proper perspective. It will help you see how blessed you really are.

What makes God's strengths so glorious is that He can do so much with so little, and a whole lot with nothing.

There may be a gulf between your 'want it' and your 'want to'. A 'want it' is the talk about the desired, drawing lots of listeners. A 'want to' is the walk to achieve its reality, and worth watching.

I DECLARE. . . I will not fear, stress, worry, or be anxious, because I know God is with me.

ACTS 16:31 ~ Believe on the Lord Jesus Christ, and you will be saved, you and your household.

NOTES & OBSERVATIONS. . .

DAY 33

GOD Is Never Tired, Weary Or Weak.

The LORD will guide you continually and
satisfy your soul in drought, and make
your bones strong. You shall be like
a watered garden, like a spring of
water, whose waters do not fail.

Isaiah 58:11

PRAYER: Father, You've accepted me and
approved me! You've empowered me to do
what You've created for my purpose. It is by
Your grace that my strength is enabled. My
need for You is in every minute of my life!

Have Your way, O God, and keep me from
standing in my way or preventing my doing
Your will. Please go before me, set my feet
on those things You've planned for me and
my future. Lord, I offer all my thanks, all of
me, in that Name, Jesus. . .

SOMETIMES. . . what we believe doesn't remotely line up with what we see or feel, nor what we have in mind or hand.

We get a little nervous in the service when we're seeing night-mares in the daytime, feeling like an orphan left at a bus stop without a token, and living life in retrograde. Self-talk tells us we 'thought' we knew God! Besides all that inner-fear-ance, not a single (or married) person has bothered to answer one call, or any question. 'Yikes' is our fave faith-ish expression.

It's not easy reading torn, worn out pages of the Bible, hands trembling, with stress our new 'plus one'. Finding the courage to look up to the hills, instead of out at the mess right in front of us, is a formidable task, as is deep breathing. Could it be this faith thing is not like we pictured it? Was there some fine print unread in our read that went unnoticed or unexplained?

Deep breathing *does* help to calm down and think. We need it big to take in the breaking news: Faith does not match reality! We must *decide* to believe, despite the visuals and the fear, and proceed on our walk of faith without any investment of in-tellect or reason, sight or feelings. Rogue!

What's really bold, vested faith in God operates in the super-natural realm as a superseder of its opponents, being superior to the factuals of the natural realm. Faith doesn't deny these factors, but it is not governed by them. Yep, Rogue-er!

Our decision to believe God and what He said, up in the face of opposing circumstances, challenging people, plus noisome pestilence, will stand when we stand up in faith found in God. That faith is what the enemy of our soul is after because that faith is connected to God, the Opponent and Enemy of all our enemies. The decision to believe Him queues us up to win the match with grace to spare, and a big fat pennant!

Yes, it's so hard to be frolicking with fun when painful realities taunt us to tears. But our faith in God and what He's said isn't in vain, nor does it return void when we believe in and rely on His intentions to *always* love and bless us. It's the root of the reason we can rest in Him (Hebrews 4:1-3, 11). His promises and faithfulness are forever truth, and for certain!

We *can* trust God to help us, for He is a good Father Who has told us to cast all our care on His shoulders because He cares for us (twice texted: Psalm 55:22, 1 Peter 5:7). He will help us *at all times*, causing us to never fail nor topple into ruin.

In the middle of the difficulties enshrouding the realities we encounter, our thanks to God give Him permission to lean in and mess with whatever or whoever dares mess with us. Allowing Him to be at the center of our focus and faith, dispelling all our fears, we can be confident to faithe in God, the King of kings, the Lord of lords, and the awesome Rogue of rogues!

SOME PEOPLE. . . are saved but live their lives the same way they did before they met Jesus.

They live *not free*, with behavioral struggles, secular mentalities, and worldly lifestyles. They still live in the ol' neighborhood of their former, familiar, and same-o same-o surroundings, even though they don't physically dwell there.

They 'met' Jesus, like you may have met a star sports figure, or the cast members of some play you enjoyed. You probably got an autograph but you didn't get the person. They 'sorta' met Jesus, but they didn't 'get' Him fa' real!

To *get* something implies you understood it cognitively, or you got what you bought at the market. You got the car washed, or your teeth cleaned, and actually have what you got. But as for this people, in their halted profile, they don't have Him yet.

What's missed out on, in the crazy good phenomenon of getting to meet Jesus, is He gets you first. He already knows you so well, for He's had His eye on you forever. Never imposing but impressive, He's hard not to take with you. These optics are intensely staggering! For His love is seen, pouring out of a sparkling eyed, radiant, smiling face, and is as cool as a summer's rain, but totally without the humidity.

To consider this God Guy with all eyes on you is breathtaking! No mind can fully imagine His wonderful-ness! It's an experience demanding a response difficult to express in words, but the soul and the spirit are caught up by its profound effects. How does one respond to such an awesome moment without transforming, growing and developing exponentially, as the impact of this meet-up saturates the encountered?

Another name for the incomparable ah-ha moment is conversion. Any true God encounter never leaves anyone the same. It's clearly more than reasonable to surmise once you become a butterfly, you will never resort to crawling again.

For those who return to where they were, to their ol', same-o, too-low-ceilings-to-allow-flying neighborhoods, you might ask, 'How's that working for you?' Point being, life is way too short to miss out on it! Why waste this swell gift Jesus died so well to give us, and that exceeding abundantly (John 10:10)?

The opportunity to meet a new day is an immeasurable grace. How much more the opportunity to meet the Creator of every day, and of all time? He is God, Who desires to be met and received in every heart and life. It is nice to respect and acknowledge others' choices. It's even nicer to pray they choose the life that's in the meeting and 'getting' God, not to mention the supra-greatness He is, has, and so loves to share!

SOME THOUGHTS. . .

The first change necessary in our followship with Jesus is the denial of 'self'. This means dismantling *our* ways and thinking. It requires abandoning our own understanding. It calls for moving out of our 'set' places of automatics, and immobilizing the venues of our norms, usuals, cozies, and familiars. John 3:30, a Text to us all: He must increase, but I must decrease.

It's complex, but not complicated. The Good News broadcasts God's all sufficient grace (ours for the asking), that impassions us to selflessly follow Jesus in mindful pursuit. Our surrender to it is the gate grace enters to woo us to commitment!

Interim blessings are a fabulous gesture of kindness from God! They have great value and much wisdom attached.

Encouraging us to be grateful, they are God's love and present help in our times of need. As signposts reminding us we are on the right track, they hold just enough supply to sustain us in difficulty, or through challenging seasons or situations.

It's important not to become satisfied with interim blessings by getting too comfortable with the welfare they embody. They are but a temporary taste of God's everlasting goodness, while being a salient segue to our next level, and a lifter of expectations. Thank God, again and again, from Whom all blessings flow!

I DECLARE. . . I love the Lord because He saved my life, and He daily keeps me from defeat and failure.

JOHN 14:21a ~ The person who has My commandments and keeps them is the one who really loves Me.

NOTES & OBSERVATIONS. . .

_____

_____

_____

_____

_____

_____

_____

_____

_____

_____

_____

_____

_____

_____

DAY 34

GOD Answers Whosoever Believes Him
And Calls On His Name.

Look at the birds of the air; they neither
sow nor reap nor gather into barns, and
yet your heavenly Father feeds them.
Are you not of more value than they?
Matthew 6:26

PRAYER: Father, I put all my trust in You,
knowing You are trustworthy. I cast all my
cares on You knowing You care about me.
I believe in You and Your faithfulness.

God, I run to You, for I know there's no way,
no one, nor any other place able to sustain
me. I look to You, my Father and my Friend,
my always forever Help. Your great names
are my sure and only hope. I honor You, my
Lord. I praise You, I thank You, in the name
above all names, Jesus. . .

SOMETIMES. . . the works of our hands become our idols. The big problem with that is having idols is sin. Further info to ruminate, idols cause our purpose to become idle.

Sin is a snare yet so easy to do. Sin is self-inflicted nonsense that courts our ego, edging God out, while disabling purpose. It's the reason Lucifer got fired and ousted from Heaven, when he could have been a contender for so much more.

Sin's payoff, death row (Romans 6:23), smears our character and disfigures the divine image of God within us. It greatly diminishes our potential to be credible and effective stewards of God's purposes, and His abundant life benefits package.

When the works of our hands, what we do, acquire or accomplish, become our idols, our sin turns into boasting. For starts, all boasts should be rendered to God Who gave us hands and the ability to use them. Creative expressions of our talents or giftings happen not solely by our own cleverness, but by the outflow of God's ability within us. It's all God, the Creator, and His creative graces working through us out loud.

Whenever we birth something noteworthy, such as innovative ideas that change lives or help children, we become a conduit through which God speaks, the vessel by which He is visibly seen. The fact we were chosen to 'co-create' with God is surely a plausible reason to be in constant awe of Him, with never ending gratitude for His consideration of trust.

We're compelled to become prodigals returned to our senses by our attention given to these Text Messages of torrid truth: Jeremiah 9:23-24 Let not the wise man boast in his wisdom, let not the mighty man boast in his might, let not the rich man boast in his riches, but let him who boasts boast in this, that he understands and knows Me, that I am the Lord... For in these things I delight, declares the Lord.
Job 31:24-28 Did I set my heart on making money, or worship at the bank? Did I boast about my wealth, show off because I was well-off? Was I ever so awed by the sun's brilliance... the moon's beauty that I let myself be seduced by them and worshiped them on the sly? If so, I would deserve the worst of punishments, I would be betraying God Himself.
Psalm 113:5-6 Who is like the Lord our God, Who dwells on high, Who humbles Himself to behold *the things** that are in the heavens and in the earth?

* Since God humbles Himself *to consider us* in His earth, can we humble ourselves *to remember* Who He is - God, and He made us? Allowing the works of our hands to become our idols is making the creation greater than the Creator. Only He is the Lord, our Maker, our Father, and Forgiver. O thank God, Who doesn't get mad when we become forgetters!

SOME PEOPLE. . . who are new to Christianity and God, are like a blind man in a new house. The idea of a new life in Christ is as unfamiliar to them as the unnerving reality of the unknown territory is to the blind man.

The unsighted can only survive by *deciding* to reach out and know the peculiar parameters of the new space. He steps to learn and sense the new grounds. Groping in the dark is common practice to him, but on this unlearned, untrodden, foreign floor, his footing is unsure, awkward, and timidly tentative. His new land doesn't 'feel' good or easy, just yet.

This scenario parallels a new life in Christ which is also peculiar. It's a bit awkward, like learning new language in a foreign land. But as exciting as it is, it can be just as challenging to handle God's mores while unhanding our lessers.

Becoming teachable is becoming willing to unlearn old ways to learn new ones. Things that *were* acceptable are now lacking, and not as good as God's goods. Until people know what His idea of good is, they will often keep a grip on what is not enough. Admitting insufficiency was never a thought for they hardly imagined the magnitude of God's extravagant heart. The joy of freedom is untold to those who never knew they'd been in bondage. So enter Jesus, and the splendor He brings to their new life table. It's holy 'wow' time on a regular basis!

New life in Christ is a never-passed-this-way-before grace. Its wealth is to contend for, to take hold of, to cherish, to grow into, to never cease from seeking and becoming more by it. It's compelling without imposing, complex yet simplistic. It will drive you from limitation, and urge you to possibility. It's a safe passage through life's nasty norms, and their melange of madness and mayhem. New life in Christ is God's love in your face.

Rather than a subjection to wondering, listening is a wonderful employ to get to know God's voice and His Word. By His kindred, merciful father-heart, He navigates a whosoever's every step to the places of His spoken design and purpose, prospering each move forward. On the journey to discovering God, a 'new lifer' will find He is superb at not letting anyone stay blind, but only if one is willing to see. For He is gracious to extend *the choice* to be healed, to follow, and to be blessed!

In the awkward stages of getting acquainted with Him and His new life, God gently leads people to His paths. He woos them to desire becoming who He created them to be. A Benefactor Who will not abandon or forsake, His mind is always on them, and His hand is never lifted from them. His love is everlasting, unchanging, unconditional, and so undeserved, but altogether their's for the asking, and the receiving. New life in Christ is a forever gift that keeps on giving and living. It's an offer not to be refused or missed! It's cool, revitalizing, Living Life Water!

SOME THOUGHTS. . .

Seek God with all your heart! You will find Him, yourself, and new dimensions of your life far exceeding all you knew before.

Once we yield to God's Lordship, taking our position in Him, we can't *stay* mad, sad, bad, rude, or crude.

Rejoice for the beginnings that don't seem big enough, for the battles that haven't overcome you, and for the beat downs that didn't break you down. Your best is *set* to come!

Those considered to be brilliant should pray for the wisdom to bring out their shine.

There will always be conflict when you attempt to match the exceptional with the ordinary.

Detachment is simply letting go of the old in-operables to take hold of the new, functioning operations.

Remand your focus to God's love for you.

I Declare. . . Today I will praise God for never leaving me empty, without, alone or abandoned.

Isaiah 41:13 ~ For I, the Lord your God, will hold your right hand, saying to you, Fear not, I will help you.

Notes & Observations. . .

DAY 35

GOD Pours Out Grace On His People
To Be No Longer Poor.

Have mercy on me, O God, according
to Your lovingkindness, according to
the greatness of Your compassion,
blot out my transgressions.
Psalm 51:1

PRAYER: O Lord, I thank You that You
have forgiven my inconsiderations and
inconsistencies. Will You please renew
me, and give me a right heart to desire
right attitudes? I need Your eyes to see
well, and with proper perspective.

I thank You, God, for a fresh start and a
new beginning everyday. You have cast
my past behind me. My heart overflows
with gratitude. I set my face forward, my
focus is You, Lord, in Jesus' name. . .

SOMETIMES. . . we commit to obeying God, sorta! We're obedient-ish. We kinda do what He says. We re-sort His commands to accommodate our preferences, politics, plans, preconceived notions, and other personal, crazy stuff.

We mostly 'go there', permitting our humanistic proclivities to dictate our spiritual responsibilities, while excusing ourselves from reasonable service to God. Whether we're not 'feelin' it', or think it's not that bad to 'jes' say no' to God's ways and desires, we are wack! We enter into a rebellion our flesh and, of course, the devil get in cahoots for an unholy triumph. Scary!

In Luke 5:4-6, we find Jesus asking Peter, who had fished unsuccessfully all night, to let down his nets, again. Peter, hesitant and exhausted, responded to His request by letting down *a net*, not nets. The haul of fish was so great it broke the net, resulting in Peter having to ask other fishers to help.

What would have happened if Peter had done exactly what Jesus asked him to do? Maybe no broke net, no need to be embarrassed over 'I told you so, dude', no splits on the fish? Peter didn't obey Jesus completely, kinda like we do.

So much for partial obedience! Add to that erroneous thinking and behavior, delayed obedience - simply doing what we got in mind when *we decide* we got time. So not nice or cool!

Partial, incomplete, or delayed obedience equals a wrong answer buzzer! God deserves our complete commitment to total obedience, entirely motivated by our love for and faith in Him. Obedience will always produce God's nod, and more of what we need, plus, some of what we desire on the side!

Evidence of this is in John 21:4-6. Standing on the seashore, Jesus asked the disciples, out in their boats, if they had any fish. They, *not recognizing Him*, said 'No!'. He then told them, 'cast your *net* on the right side, you'll find some'. When they did, a huge amount of fish were caught. Without knowing who He was, they obeyed. We know, but don't obey! The result of their immediate obedience was a huge supply of fish, exactly what they needed! In Verse 11, we discover, miraculously, the *net was not broken* by the overflowing, huge haul of large fish.

If we relent from doing our version of godly behavior, and repent from every action that could appear as disobedience, we will experience an overflow, a great haul, of God's generosity. As recompense for our faithful obedience, He'll supply every grace in every place of our need and concern. Consider well: Deuteronomy 1:19 If you are willing and obedient, you will
eat the best of the land. Obey and get a bonus!
1 Peter 1:14 Be obedient to God, and do not allow your lives to be shaped by those desires you had when you were still ignorant. Thank God His love is so patient and kind!

SOME PEOPLE. . . love principles more than the reasons they were established. To them, godly principles are more fun to follow than Jesus, the Author of principle!

Back in the day, their tag could've been 'pharisee'. Now, they slink behind religious rule, or denominational dictates, as their personal lean to for being right rather than righteous. Perhaps, they are proponents of an image of Christianity that sidesteps the reality of Jesus Christ Who is *the* image and person of real Christianity. Unfortunately, an image of an ideal or concept is only a billboard without words or information.

It takes courage to want and to do better. In part, the problem of this people is thinking they're 'jes' fine'. They refuse to take on the challenge of a new thought. Obliviously, the picture on a cake box is better than making a cake. No carbs, please!

Christianity embodies the component of responsibility to conviction's conversion. It comes with the territory. It's the ultimate change - transformation, into the image of Jesus Christ, after Whom Christianity is named. No other name is attached which simplifies following after Jesus. It helps avoid the confusion of running after some Jesse, John, or Jane, who almost, maybe, kinda, sorta looks a lot like Him. Thank God He can heal blind eyes to see who, or Who is The Real Deal!

In our personal process of transitioning, if we remain focused on Jesus, following close, change will draw less and less resistance. When we're better sighted and more decisive, religion will no longer precede us. This move forward looses us from religion, like a pardon releases one from prison!

Since Christianity is a confronter, we can't mistake it for a conformer to our ways. God's Holy Spirit will comfort us in our difficulty, but Christianity won't shrink wrap itself to make us comfortable in our issues. It draws us out of our self-indulgence to form us into Christ's virtuous image. It gives us an authentic relationship with God. What *was* us is no match for God with us, and within us. No other religion can nor offers to do that.

We all like 'lookin' good'! But it's better to be good with God on the inside than to look good with a world of religious ideologies on the outside. It's the how that defines the why of real Christianity. It's the way to stay connected to God, and to function in the power of being believable Believers. It is the 'want to' of demonstrating God's will to save and deliver us all from error, ourselves, and a very hot hell. It's His principle!

2 Corinthians 3:18 As the Spirit of the Lord works within us, we become more and more like Him. Religion and religious people are so close, but need a push into the everlasting, forever loving arms of Jesus. Ah ha! It's Intercession Time!

SOME THOUGHTS. . .

Complacency is a seduction that sits us down, shuts us up,
and uses a dimmer on our light in the world.

God has given us salvation - His eternal rescue plan!
His intention is that we're helped out of and delivered from
the depravity of the world. It's His plan that we might be prepared, anointed and equipped, and then sent by Him to affect the world and its culture.

Salvation's call to us is an assignment to engage the world to
God by invitation: #1. To know His love, #2. To experience His
power in their lives, and #3. To know Him in relationship.

This gift of salvation comes with another gift called grace. It's
an extremely sufficient enabling to do what God, the Caller
and Savior, helped and delivered us for. He will make fruitful
and prosperous any whosoever daring enough to answer the
call, accomplish the assignment, and accept the invite.

Adolescent people can be a real challenge to deal with,
especially when they're over 40.

When trouble is deep-seated and long standing, try kneeling.

I DECLARE. . . As Jesus is, so am I: Committed, faithful, loving, holy, healthy, wealthy, wise, obedient, strong, and effective.

PROVERBS 21:21 ~ He who pursues righteousness and love will find life, prosperity, and honor.

NOTES & OBSERVATIONS. . .

_____

_____

_____

_____

_____

_____

_____

_____

_____

_____

_____

_____

_____

_____

_____

DAY 36

God Holds Your Hand And Keeps Your Life.

Your ears will hear a word behind you,
saying, "This is the way, walk in it,"
when you turn to the right hand
or when you turn to the left.

Isaiah 30:21

PRAYER: God, I will honor You in every room of my life. Light my path, my Jesus, for You are the Light of the world. Shine, Almighty God! Hold me up so I won't slip and fall into things less than my purpose, or that may hinder my efforts forward.

Please change me and my mind, my will and appetites, and the ways of my heart. I confess, Lord, You are the Center of my life, and the Desire of my soul. Walk with me, and steady my steps to follow You. I give You thanks, my Jesus. . .

SOMETIMES. . . it gets really dark outside, and inside, too. Because of our ol' pal and brother, Adam, darkness and its lil' buddy, sin, can surround us. But our faithful Friend and Father, God, doesn't want us stuck with dark feelings of dismay, anxiety and stress, or to become distraught by vanishing hope.

God calls us to remember our hope is not in the world or any conditions, nor is it based on people. Our hope is in Him Who is The Way, The Truth, and The Life. He is The Light, brighter and more radiant than the sun which, by the way, He made!

We can answer that call to rise up and come to standing into His marvelous Light. There we see to know, with confidence and clarity, who we are amidst dark times and seasons.

It's a decision, prompted by faith in an unfailing God, to place our lives, our future, our cares, and our hope in His more than capable hands. Besides *being* our hope, He's got great plans to prosper us, to give us His peace and confidence, His future and hope for an expected, well lit end (Jeremiah 29:11).

God holds the heavens, the earth, and all of us. He's a meticulously loving Caregiver. We can doubtlessly believe, trust and hope in Him. We can chill and de-stress in His loving arms for we know our security is in Him and His care alone. He made us to be His own dear, dependent lil' kids (Galatians 3:26)!

SOME PEOPLE. . . haven't fully acclimated to the higher level of their anointing, their call, or their position in life. Time plays a role, as does discipline, and a decided 'want to'.

There is a mandatory adjustment to their mindsets, actions, and conversations. Needed, too, is purposeful, positive, and spiritual self-talk to enlighten, encourage, and empower.

For sure, they are called and appointed to be a chef, a parent, or a senator. But realignment of the soul - mind, will and emotions, is a prerequisite to amend and enhance behavioral, experiential, and educational practices and prowess. It's the prosthesis to fair well in any stalwart effort toward success in reaching loftier levels of the appointment entrusted to them. With excellent preparation, the discipline of mind change, the focus to thrive, and the synergistic agreement of these fundamentals, no doubt, they are destined to become exceptional.

Ceding to these transformings affects patterns of living, loving, thinking, and performing. In their process of turning, in the steps of that ascension, they will rise to see and to know the higher dimension is where God lives and blesses.
Isaiah 57:15 Thus says the High and Lofty One, Who inhabits eternity, Whose name is Holy: Though I live high above in the holy place, I am here to help those who are humble and depend only on Me.

SOME THOUGHTS. . .

Everywhere our feet tread has tutorial opportunities along the path of process. They are handfuls of purpose that prepare us, teach and equip us: #1. To become what we've been predestined to be, #2. To receive what God has predetermined us to possess, and #3. To perform what God has purposed us to do.

Unbelief doesn't change Jesus' power, nature or abilities. But it can prevent unbelievers from experiencing all He does.

Pride and arrogance are perverted confidence.

God will not bless who you pretend to be, nor will He heal what you deny, hide, or hide behind.

If your spirituality doesn't impact and inform your daily life, you may be engaging a religious hobby.

God is not contained within the frame of our past experiences with Him, or our present knowledge of Him. He calls us closer to know the God we don't know yet, for His love is ever seeking its deeper expression, and a greater relationship with us.

I DECLARE. . . Lord, I submit to You, Your will, and Your ways.

2 SAMUEL 22:37 ~ You provide a broad path for my feet so that my ankles do not give way.

NOTES & OBSERVATIONS. . .

DAY 37

God Chose You For Himself, And He Made You To Be His Own Child.

Love means following His commandments,
and His unifying commandment is that
you conduct your lives in love.
2 John 1:6a

PRAYER: Abba Father, You are the God
of my strength and courage. You are with
me when I'm not turned to You. Your eyes
are on me while my focus is far off.

Lord, please adjust my sights. Help me to
be more conscious of You than the things
around me making me fearful, distracted,
and forgetting You and who I am to You. I
love You, God! I yield my heart, my being,
my soul, and all that I am to You. I pray in
Your name, Lord Jesus. . .

SOMETIMES. . . you need to investigate what you believe, how you came to that belief, and why you believe it.

A quality-of-faith control check will keep you from succumbing to the pressure, or embarrassment, of: #1. Not knowing the premise of the faith journey you're on, and #2. Whether or not what or who you're banking on (believing) is credible enough to make a good return on your faith's investment.

For consideration, God, the Creator of the universe and you, alone promises an amazing life, pardon of sins and mistakes, a forever covenant of unconditional love, plus, eternal life at His House, Heaven. It's all yours *if you decide* to believe Him, and fully receive what He's promised and has to offer.

FYI, God always makes good on His Word, upholding it above His name (Psalm 138:2). He's the sole Guarantor of everything He says and does. Your faith, when planted in the faithfulness and power of His Word, His flawless track record and His truth, which He is, will never be fruitless, disappointed, or void.

Planting seeds of faith in any other ideal, premise, person, belief, or religious doctrine can leave you short on return. At the end of the day, it's all good and profitable to believe in an all good, all the time great God, Who believes in you! Besides, Jesus did say, "Have faith in God" (Mark 11:22)!

SOME PEOPLE. . . perceive themselves as awesome, spiritual giants, and so holy! They are consumed on account of all their doings and much rule keeping, assuming their godly-ish performances justify being a bit stand-offishly highbrow.

Because they're of this ilk, the need to surrender to worship is not required in their regimen of ritual. At the root of this self-deception is an old, infectious malady causing spiritual dementia. Its real name is getting-too-familiar-with-God, or, GTFWG. It's the disease that got Lucifer a pink slip, and so fire-d.

The side effect of spiritual dementia, like amnesia's lost memory, is forgetfulness of identity, where you are, how you arrived, or the details of other vital components of one's existence. Its manifestation mimics arrogant ignorance, another debilitating, iniquitous, spiritual and social infirmity.

GTFWG people abandon humility in the throes of forgetting everything they've been forgiven of. They can't remember all they have or have received. In fact, it isn't uncommon for the infected to plagiarize gifts and graces of God as if they were self-generated, or greatly deserved. Fear of God is forsaken!

It's no surprise GTFWG sufferers fail availing worship. As a tremendous therapy toward recovery, worship draws one's focus away from self, enabling surrender to God. Yielding to do so releases the power of God's presence to pour into every deficit of the soul. That's where healing begins! That's where new paths of possibility open the place impossibilities once closed up, halting the flow of real life and true spirituality.

In that supernatural space of worship, the elixir of holy wholeness, giving what humanity yields to receive, is lethal weaponry against darkness. Light and lightness lift antithetical factors off and out of the path forward. Merging the divinity of the Father with the frailty of the child makes the miraculous manifest. New, unuttered before words are oft silently spoken. Unheard before psalmody, erupting from deep within the soul, is a now song. How great the moment for how great is He!

Moments of worship, in spirit and in truth, are times of refreshing, times of mind renewal, times of coming to one's senses once disheveled by distraction. These moments are the meds needed to supplant unholy affections and appetites from their lurings to replant them in God, the Healer. He's the only Spirit alive with freedom, and, of course, escape from GTFWG.

Holy wholeness is the result of God encounters. It's a knowing, never a familiarity. God rearranges us, and our furniture, drawing us closer to know Him by heart, and to be as He is. In surrender to worship, we become the platform of His Presence, conjoined as one with Him, and all the more His own!

SOME THOUGHTS. . .

Praise God for the day, while you were lost, Jesus died on the cross, making a way out of no way for you to be saved, found, rescued, forgiven, and so loved by Him forever!

Never be intimidated! The best are no better than you, and the worst are no less than you.

Faith is a decision to triumph over reason and impossibility.

It's only human to want to know God a bit before you commit, but it's wisdom to commit to know Him.

The challenges that confront the heart can bring disclosure and correction to its motives and agenda.

There comes a time when you need to cease from trying to convince those who refuse to be convinced.
Choose to stay in peace, decide to pray for them, and trust God with them and for their conviction.

Worship when you fast for faster results.

I DECLARE. . . I believe God delights in me, and in making prosperous all the works of my hands.

DANIEL 6:27a ~ He is a Savior and Deliverer! He works signs and wonders in the heavens and on the earth.

NOTES & OBSERVATIONS. . .

DAY 38

GOD's Transforming Power Is In The Peace And Joy Of His Presence!

Come to Me, all you who labor and are
heavy laden, and I will give you rest.
Matthew 11:28

PRAYER: Dear God, I am counting on
You for all I need. It seems my storage
is empty, but I am available to You and
Your restoration of my heart and soul.

Father, You're abundantly able in supply
and availability, in kindnesses, peace, in
generosity and loving care. My thanks to
You is endless for You love me, hear me,
and answer my calls constantly. My God,
for all these graces, I'll love You forever!
In Jesus' magnificent, powerful, healing,
holy, amazing name, I pray. . .

SOMETIMES. . . we get caught up in our messes, setting the stage for our major and many stresses.

Why is that? We do church, most of, well, some of the time. We pray and meditate, though we miss a couple of few days. At least traffic is no longer a reason to employ ye ol' sign language, 'cause we're walkin' by faith, in Jesus' name!

But the messes keep on messing with us. Is God mad about something we did or didn't do? Does He not like us? It's frightful figuring it all out. Whining over the why's adds to the agita.

Hey, messes happen! It's the flesh suit that has a tendency to be a mess magnet. We can defect, yielding to a lay down in those prescribed green pastures. Or, let's try covering up with God's peace surpassing all our misunderstanding!

Regardless of the bate of the crazies pulling us to the left, we can clean up our messes with God-nesses! How 'bout a few big gulps of His peacefulness, faithfulness, forgiveness, goodness, kindness, loveliness, and His ain't-He-alright-ness?

God promises to cover our sins and shame. Will He not cover, by His Father-ness, the messes we got pushed or stumbled into? We gotta put on His Christ-nesses over our minds and our messes, to taste and see how He blesses, de-stresses, and refreshes, on a regular basis! O Yes-ness!

SOME PEOPLE. . . vehemently and passionately abhor the thought, concept and idea of trying something new.

To consider 'different' becomes an overwhelming elephant in the room they decide to look over and around to avoid acknowledging it, or their need to engage and respond to it.

The new, next thing is usually more and surely better than the ol' accustomed to thing they hold onto with a pit bull grip. Yet, while clutching the oldie-but-not-so-goodie, they complain of its flaws, and the constant trouble of its not-so-usefulness.

To them, to reach out of their so-called comfort zone is hazardously more inconvenient than the inconvenience of the no-op thing(s) surrounding them. Another avoidance is learning God cannot give what is not received. Like a crying, hungry baby, their complaints are great, but no attempt is made to get that fresh milk, that grace, pouring out from His hand.

God's mercies are new every morning! They are the wake up call to get in alignment and agreement with Him. They are the help to let go and leave behind the old. *When* this people shift to see the now and the new, they will be able to reach for and receive the present, purposed, and fresh plans of God.

Yielding *to reach* is the premise for God's promises coming to pass, and for a fresh new to enter the room, exit elephant.

SOME THOUGHTS. . .

Growth is understanding what happened to you in your past will always be a factor, but it won't always be a hurt.

Think on the truth of Romans 12:10: Love one another with brotherly affection, as family members, giving precedence and showing honor to one another.

Love and honor are keys that render tremendous returns in diverse places because they display God big in us. When we aim to be generous with our love and honor, God generously gives Himself and His favor to us. This Text Message is worthy of heeding if we want to receive what God wants to give.

Alignment with God is the ticket to every place you must go, and the proviso to sustain you there.

Without faith, it is impossible to please God.
With worship, it is possible to delight His heart!

Change is God's way to keep us new, fresh, and relevant.

False perceptions of yourself incarcerate your true identity.

I DECLARE. . . I will not be moved by any circumstances that
would distract me from my focus on Jesus.

PSALM 18:30 ~ As for God, His way is perfect; the word of the
LORD is proven; He is a shield to all who trust in Him.

NOTES & OBSERVATIONS. . .

DAY 39

GOD Is The Same Yesterday, Today And Forever.
He Changes Not For He Is Perfect!

Truly I have spoken; truly I will bring it to
pass. I have planned it, surely I will do it.
Isaiah 46:11b

PRAYER: My Father, I thank You for the
dreams You've placed in my heart. What
You say of me, I proclaim: I can and I will
do all You have purposed for me.

Lord, direct my mind, my strengths, and
my heart toward You and Your will. Help
me accomplish what You have designed
for my life. I am in awe You trust me with
Your plans. Please give me the capacity
and the wisdom to know and understand
what I must do daily. For all You are, and
for everything you do for me, I will praise
You, my Lord, in Jesus' name. . .

SOMETIMES. . . we just don't listen. Maybe what we hear isn't our fave flavor, and not at all a match to our mindset.

Selective hearing flows onto our prayer life, too. We ask God for help, to grace our challenges and answer our cries. But if His response isn't exactly what we wanted to hear, we pray on, turning up the volume, adding an 'O, Lord!' here and there, in hopes of receiving 'it'. We feel crushed, slighted, unattended to because God'sFulfillmentCenter.com has not sent what we had in mind for our supplicated expectation.

The problem we need to face: We missed the fact that we *did* get an answer. If we'd only get past our appetites, we may get to know the blessing of being *heard by God*. Yes, we prayed a specific prayer, with a specific answer planted firmly in our fervency. But God's 'Nope' is all bubble-wrapped and delivered in His lovingkindness. Since He knows exactly what we do and don't need, and what we can handle, He does promise to supply all that, but not those fantasized demands for our personal satieties. Slang-anese for that is, 'we be trippin'!

The real issue - our decisions, concerning our needs, wants and must haves, get decided sans God's 'OK'. If our pleas are unpleasing to His will, they may well go unmet, or unheard for response. In our haste to be in charge, since we got it goin' on, our presumption speaks before He does. We're 'en mute', so we can't hear Him say, "I do all things well-er than you".

How cool is God! In His amazing graciousness, He won't give us 'our' answer, despite the ugly-cry sessions. In part, it's because what we hoped for is *jes' for us* and our 'lookin' good 'n' holy' daze. In truth, it doesn't include much more than our desires (ouchalujah!). In reality, we can't fake it for God knows all our heart, and all we think. In fact, He knows before we know to ever verbalize any thoughts at all (uh oh!).

We've heard and hope God will bless us. However, we didn't listen to the whole sentence, nor hear with our heart His intention. The dealio is He blesses us *to be* a blessing. If His intention is omitted, we can't steward to manage the abundance of His heart, nor handle the responsibility of receiving His more.

A forever truth is Psalm 84:11 - No good thing will He withhold from us! True, too, is we've got to be aligned with Him, *for Him and His sake*, to assure His plans and our purpose happen for the good of His Name, not for us alone. If our concern is singly for the good of our show, God can't be seen or known. Who'll get to experience how great and very cool He is? But if we listen, we'll hear His sweet, intense love for us *in* all His voicings, *in* the Word, and *in* every answer to us. It's a beautiful day in the neighborhood when we have ears to actually hear!

SOME PEOPLE. . . do the right thing for the wrong reason. The outcome seems fruitful at the start, but over time, those diminishing returns indicate a not-so-wise expenditure.

Eventually, truth will turn the light on the darkness - that not-so-nice effort, AKA agenda. It's a commonality for folk seeking an easier way to get where they want to be, or do what they're trying to accomplish for 'ta-da' moments of mention and attention. Sadly, they forget God, the only Audience taking actual note of them and giving significance to their endeavors.

When that big-o halogen light of His truth spots what's not-so-right, there's no shade from flimsy excuses as to why or how error got in the room of their mind. There's no way to bypass the process to get to sustainable progress. Short cuts can become great lacerations that may hurt now and later.

Doing the right thing because it's right to do is commendable, both in effort and intention. The question to answer: Will God be honored with no added kudos to us? Self gets ousted from the agenda when we thank God for the privilege of being a resource and an example of His love, benevolence, and power.

What we do for God because we love Him, shines for eternity, and gets Him seen on us and our efforts. Momentary spotlights of notice and role-ing credits grow dim in His Light!

SOME THOUGHTS. . .

Faith considers the lock, but believes the key.

God "*makes us* to lie down in green pastures" (Psalm 23:2) to
renew and refill us, to refresh and restore us, remaking us to
His original design of cool.

It's one thing to read and study the Word of God, however,
it's quite another to believe it.

On every journey toward birthing greater will come opposition,
distractions, and interruptions to test our faith, and to question
our qualifications for entering the next level.
Be stayed, focused, and breathe through the labor pains.

The law of reciprocity is the law of increase. In other words,
you will reap as you give from all you are given.

We must *grow through* what we go through! If not, we won't
have the faith, hope, peace and joy, nor depth of experience
to testify of God's goodness and His mighty power that were
accessed to us, but not fully utilized by us.

I DECLARE. . . I will trust God because He is my Father. I will follow His lead, believing that His Word is love and truth.

JEREMIAH 17:7 ~ Blessed is the one who believes, trust, and relies on the LORD, and whose hope and confidence the LORD is.

NOTES & OBSERVATIONS. . .

DAY 40

GOD Is The Helper Of The Fatherless, The Outcast,
The Forsaken, The Hopeless, And The Helpless.

By awesome deeds in righteousness You
will answer us, O God of our salvation, You
Who are the confidence of all the ends
of the earth, and of the far off seas.

Psalm 65:5

PRAYER: O Lord, my God, and my Father!
You are more than I know! You consider me
and love me. You know my voice. With Your
compassion, You hear me call Your name!

I will listen for Your voice speaking the truth
I need to hear. I long for You daily! You took
me out from troubles and saved my life. For
this, my Lord, for regarding me as Your own,
I bless You, I thank You, and I praise You, in
Jesus' Almighty name. . .

SOMETIMES. . . accomplishing The Dream, that vision in our heart, can be so hard. Like a Mount Everest expedition, it's a far distance to reach, and just as far in height to climb.

Where did that dream come from anyway? Is it a delusion, a sci-fi movie impartation, or was it that burger just before bed? And why does it reoccur, haunting us in quiet times, confusing times, minding our own business times, baiting our desire and attention? We begin to imagine it more and more, in 3-D, surround sound, wide-screen, and in unbelievable detail.

When we least expect it, in echo mode, we hear, 'I *can* do all things through Christ...' (Philippians 4:13). In the recesses of our mind, it also reoccurs to us that it is God Who gives to us dreams of significance. So then, it must be God Who *has to* make our dreams happen, right? O yes, confirmation!

In the process of the dream becoming a visual reality, we do have a responsibility to mount if we're to see and experience it in living color. That translates to our genuine passion, availability, and commitment to its full, vibrantly alive production!

The previews in our mind are simply trailers of what God projected on the screen of our purpose from the beginning of all time. His plans and intentions were long before we were. The dream is God's broadcast of an impossibility onto a doable -

a visual of His heart. *We* get to co-produce and co-create with the Creator of all purpose and every great dream!

Way, way back in the day, when Joseph dreamed, though opposed and challenged, his dreams came to pass. The pharaoh of his challenge dreamed a dream only Joseph could interpret and turn to favor for himself, his family, and all of Egypt.

When King Nebuchadnezzar dreamed, Daniel unraveled what the king couldn't. We dream dreams that prophesy relevance to the signs of our times. Wisdom warns not to become or follow dreamers who cast visions that turn us to distraction from God or purpose. For God alone is The Dream Maker of kaleidoscopic, unparalleled imagery, and intended forth telling.

Dreams, divinely crafted by God, will come to birth. Every real dream is an indelible, imparted view of God's heart. Each one is born from His mind's inimitable creativity and incomparable artistry, and is superbly ladened with purpose.

As awe-striking, overwhelming, and formidable as our dream may well be, we must remember to thank God! Firstly, for His trusting us with it. Secondly, for allowing us to usher the projected visual of His mind into a major moment, divinely orchestrated for and supernaturally credited to our purpose. Thirdly, for the faith to project His heart, in full view, on our life screen!

SOME PEOPLE. . . need a lot more courage to shift their paradigms than they have in their backpacks. It always takes great courage, faith, and determination to move forward!

Whether it's a new hair color, eliminating analog for digital, or updating that outdated wardrobe, there are more than a few items to tackle toward an orderly shift. First is deciding what to consider as priority and essential on that Gotta Do List.

Much of the same intentional thought, if not more, applies to renewing the ways, habits, thoughts, and modus operandi of 'self' for one's personal or spiritual paradigm. It's a huge decision to get loosed from the shackles of the familiars and the forevers, to brave the climb up a new day fully loaded with forwarding wisdoms, and excitingly fresh explores.

Beyond The List are even more decisions: *To see* the light in a higher wattage; *To choose* living a life greater than the one too many are accustomed to living lesser, or as usual; *To become* a person of efficacious influence, purposed by God.

A spiritual paradigm shift is an awakening to new truth. It's an entry to the knowledge and hope of God's calling us out of *our* world into His Kingdom. It's a new beginning, an upright landing, right in the middle of His reasons and will as to why we're on the planet. And, it can be an abrupt eye-opener.

Like a nightmare, a shift forward can be the discovery of our scary place of uncertainty. With it comes the unknown, the uncomfortable, the unfamiliar. Add to these un's lots of huh?'s, which undo our equilibrium of cool to not even a trace.

In every deep breath, in every attempt to yield, in every effort to get past every reason to remain tethered to our formerlies, is God's gentle nudge. Twinkling, illumining light is His accompaniment. In it, the attraction of the what was's that worked so well before begins to fade like mist. If we dare resist the beauty of His persistent urging into the process forward, as unnerving and provokingly didactic as it is, we'll miss our cue - His call to answer our greatest emerging.

Let's not pass up God's bypass from antiquity to a beyond all measure more, that is, His exceeding abundantly above imaginings purposed for His own. Our past experiences, astute learnings, and renown accomplishments are as nothing compared to the mind, heart, and intentions of God's plan for us.

It takes courage to put aside what cannot meet the 'great' within us waiting to appear, to step up to new heights never before ascended. Begone, ye phone booth of yore! "Bye!", aluminum foiled antenna, and ye ol' mindset. Today announces a tomorrow we were so born for! With an ever-increasing faith, say, "Hello, and yes!" to the bigger, better, and new shift forward!

SOME THOUGHTS. . .

Because He delights in our prosperity - progress, growth, increase, and good success (Psalm 35:27), God absolutely so loves to do for us what we cannot do. How-so-never, He will not do for us what we can but don't do for ourselves.

Avoid DUI's ~ Driving, or doing anything, under the influence of the flesh, anger, bitterness, retaliation, hatred, fear, or other negative postures that prevent sound judgment and thought.

Without the comprehension of God's love for us personally, we may experience His Word as merely an historic narrative, full of information, but not as God, Himself.

John 1:1 In the beginning was the Word, and the Word was with God, and *the Word was God.* Verse 14 reveals that the Word, Jesus, became flesh to dwell among us, coming close enough to connect and relate to us, to reconcile and free us, all by His unconditional, miraculous love.

The more we examine the Word, God's love letter, the more we encounter Him. The more we yield to know it, the better we will know God and His heart to forever love us! As a gift nearly too incomprehensible to perceive, His love, when it's received, will transform our whole life, heart and soul.

I DECLARE. . . Today I will stand in the identity and strength, the authority and power of who I am - God's child!

COLOSSIANS 3:17 ~ Whatever you do, in word or deed, do all in the name of the Lord Jesus, giving thanks to God the Father.

NOTES & OBSERVATIONS. . .

You and your purpose are invaluable!
It's because both are created by God
Who loves you, Who is for you, and
Who will be with you always.

In fact, God thinks you are so stunning,
He promises to 'rejoice over you with
loud singing'! ~ Zephaniah 3:17.

And, In Conclusion. . .

Thank you for taking this journey. It is the hope of my heart that the words, thoughts, and information herein are appropriately edifying for you, and an encouragement to expand your walk toward knowing and believing God more.

Despite the chasm between God and man, He reaches into the minuscule capacities of humanity to give Himself to us. He creates an irrefutable connecting arc to not only relate to us, but to intimately and indelibly touch our lives.

Within the heart, the reality of God comes first. There, real relationship begins. It is revelation and mystery. It is a beautiful dream becoming truer, and more exciting, the more we are impassioned to experience Him. God will bless every labor and turn to seek and find Him. Without disappointment, we will. It's in the pursuit we discover He is infinitely greater than we imagine, and more than we can contain. From His power and kindnesses, He pours depth and substance into our faithing in Him. He will light the countenance and life of anyone willing and available to behold Him!

May God and His graces amaze you more and more!

Be encouraged! You are fearfully and wonderfully made, called and chosen by God Who has equipped you with His power and purpose to do exploits. Believe, trust, and never doubt Him!

Ivory Stone

To correspond with the author, write to:

CORNERSTONE WORX
P.O. Box 4705
Valley Village, CA 91617
USA

E-mail: info@cornerstoneworx.com

Printed in the United States
By Bookmasters